CONTEMPORARY LODGING SECURITY

CONTEMPORARY LODGING SECURITY

Mark H. Beaudry

Butterworth-Heinemann
Boston Oxford Melbourne Singapore Toronto Munich New Delhi Tokyo

Library of Congress Cataloging-in-Publication Data

Beaudry, Mark.
    Contemporary lodging security / by Mark Beaudry.
        p.   cm.
    Includes bibliographical references and index.
    ISBN 0-7506-9574-9 (alk. paper)
    1. Hotels--Security measures. I. Title.
    TX911.3.S4B43   1996
    647.94'068'4--dc20   95-34236
                                     CIP

British Library Cataloguing-in-Publication Data
A catalogue record for this book is available from the British Library.

The publisher offers discounts on bulk orders of this book.
For information, please write:

Manager of Special Sales
Butterworth-Heinemann
313 Washington Street
Newton, MA 02158–1626

10 9 8 7 6 5 4 3 2 1

Printed in the United States of America

Contents

Acknowledgments

I would like to thank the following individuals for being good friends and mentors for many years: Tom Lee, Skip Brandt, Royd Bjornoy, Jim Papazian, and Mario Colangelo. Working with these talented professionals has not only been the opportunity of a lifetime, it has also been an honor and a pleasure.

I wish I could individually thank each of my countless colleagues in the lodging industry and the International Lodging Safety & Security Association, to whom I owe so much.

I would like to thank the faculty and staff, past and present, of Northeastern University's College of Criminal Justice, located in Boston, Massachusetts.

I wish to thank my mentor and friend Norman Bates, President, Liability Consultants, Framingham, Massachusetts. Finally, I would like to dedicate this book to my wife Susan and daughter Jordan, who were kind enough to allow me the time for this project.

Introduction

The term "hotel" is an all-inclusive designation for facilities that provide comfortable lodging and generally, but not always, food, beverage, entertainment, a business environment, and other "away from home" services. The term "motel" is a general designation for lodging establishments that specialize in attracting the motoring public by offering parking accommodations. The distinctions between hotels and motels are gradually disappearing, however. Motels, motor hotels, resort hotels, inns, country clubs, and conference centers are among the varieties of hotels, and the terms applied are based primarily on differences in layout and design.

Today's hotels may offer a variety of services and activities for their transient and permanent guests. A traveler who is staying at a hotel for a limited period of time is commonly described as a guest. Besides providing for lodging and meals, hotels usually have newsstands, retail shops, restaurants, cocktail lounges, health clubs, concierges, and other quality services. Generally, parking facilities are available. Some may have recreational facilities, such as saunas and swimming pools, while others may offer tennis and racquetball courts, gyms, and exercise rooms. In states where it is legal, gambling casinos may be located on the premises.

The hotel may be a high-rise building or part of a larger high-rise office complex. It may be a resort-type facility spread out over a campus-style setting offering skiing, golf, boating, horseback riding, and other activities. In recent years, conference centers offering multipurpose meeting facilities and amusement parks have become very popular. Some larger hotels today have 5,000 or more guest rooms.

Because hotels offer such diversity of facilities and activities, no one security program will fit all properties. The security program must be designed to fit the needs and characteristics of the individual hotel. While crime is not always preventable, certain policies and procedures, properly implemented, may deter or discourage criminal activity.

Therefore, as both a disclaimer and a reminder, the material contained in this book is offered as a general guide. It may not, however, be applicable to all needs. In fact, many of the issues outlined in the text will have different legal ramifications in each state or country. Legal counsel or other expert assistance should be sought if required. The author and publisher cannot assume and hereby disclaim any liability to any party for any loss or damage arising in any way from the use of this publication or any information obtained from any source contained herein.

CONTEMPORARY LODGING SECURITY

History of Lodging Security

Although it is possible to track the evolution of private security, the historical development of lodging security is more vague and difficult to trace back to a single hotel. The research does indicate, however, that the origins of lodging security go back several centuries. From the early 1400s to the 1600s, the ancient castles, palaces, and baronial mansions of Europe often offered dining and lodging accommodations to medieval knights and other travelers. Noble families, kings, and lords enjoyed residing in these secure fortresses with their fine furnishings, tapestries, paintings, mosaics, weaponry, fireplaces, and hewn stone. Today, in fact, many of the old castles throughout Europe have been tastefully adapted to receive modern guests with all the authentic details such as moats, four-poster canopied beds, and towers. Many artifacts and priceless pieces have been secured via undetectable security hardware.

In America, shortly after 1621 (the founding of Plymouth), taverns were generally among the first structures erected in colonial communities. According to Lender and Martin (p. 12) major population centers like Boston had numerous taverns (although few were licensed in the early 1600s), and even smaller towns commonly had two or more. Indeed, concern for the accommodation of travelers was so great in New England that if any village lacked an inn, authorities could direct the locality to see that one opened in the near future. Taverns filled a variety of needs. In many areas, they were the most convenient retail outlets for liquor, and often the only places where travelers could find food and lodging. They provided the surrounding regions with a forum for social interaction, which often included political, religious, and other gatherings. Before and during the Revolution, for example, inns were favorite places for political discussions, and they served as rallying points for the militia and as recruiting stations for the Continental army. Innkeepers ideally reflected the high public status accorded their establishments, and in reality they often did (Lender and Martin, pp. 12–13).

Up to about the mid-1800s, the innkeepers maintained the security of their own inns with assistance from other townspeople, statesmen, and church ministers. Sometime around the fall of 1858, Allan Pinkerton recognized that the weakness of the public police had placed the existing private police in a profitable position. He soon formed his own company to compete with these "independents." His Pinkerton Protective Patrol was a small body of uniformed watchmen who contracted with businesses to offer nighttime security (Morn, p. 29).

In the 1880s and 1890s, this changed. Generally, the public police detectives specialized in the professional criminal and the private detectives specialized in the casual criminal. In some ways professional criminals were easier to detect; criminal techniques and styles were more identifiable and predictable.

In addition to the lackluster performance of the public police, private detectives had several advantages. They could trace—and chase—crooks across the country, paying little heed to jurisdictional lines, whereas the urban police were reluctant to venture out beyond city limits. Furthermore, much private property—such as department stores, hotels, and sporting facilities—became public places in need of policing. Yet the professional thief's success depended (and still depends today) on the business community's lack of security sophistication. Banks, jewelry stores, department emporiums, and hotel rooms were all vulnerable to criminals, especially at night. The simplest of tools opened most doors in America (Morn, pp. 86–87).

During this time, one of the most important law enforcement men in the nineteenth century, Robert W. McClaughry, stated:

> The rise of the private detective agency was due to the inadequacies of the public police systems. The watchmen were useful because it was impossible to provide a police force large enough to meet all of the wants of business, and we have found that they work very well in connection with one police service. In February 1893, the Senate and House issued reports agreeing that hiring of private guards was due to the inability of public police and authority to render protection to persons and property (Morn, pp. 105–107).

The success of the private sector in fighting criminality encouraged those of a more conservative bent. The value of private detective work was reaffirmed: there was an alternative to the public police in America (Morn, pp. 115–116).

Contract security services were hired between the 1870s and the Depression of the 1930s. With few exceptions, proprietary or in-house security hardly existed before the defense-related "plant protection" boom of the early 1940s. The impetus for modern private security effectively began in that decade and it came of age only in the third quarter of the twentieth century (Fischer, p. 12).

Yet even as early as twenty years ago, many hotels considered security important enough that they had a proprietary security department within the hotel organizational chart (as opposed to hiring contract security or ignoring security alto-gether). Contemporary lodging security came about as a result of expanded operations within the hotels that began growing and facing a serious need to protect their guests and hotel assets.

It is far beyond the scope of this book to attempt to analyze or even to chronologically list all the factors involved in the trend toward increasing crime, even if we were to restrict such a study to crimes against hotels and their occupants. What is im-portant here is to make clear note of the increase and its strong impact on society's perception of safe and secure hotel environ-ments. Most significant is the realization that the sheer magni-tude of crime in our society prevents the criminal justice system by itself from adequately controlling and preventing crime.

The push toward making hotel security more professional can be observed in the proliferation of active security depart-ments as well as of trade organizations such as ASIS, ILSSA, and the AH&MA Security Committee. Yet despite the many efforts already made, there are still some who feel that major obstacles need to be overcome, and that security managers must be key members of hotels' executive committees. Fortunately, hotel owners' and senior managers' thinking is undergoing a change. The lodging industry is realizing that the adage "you get what you pay for" definitely applies to the quality of security depart-ments. This realization should, in turn, pressure the industry to upgrade the image and position of hotel security.

As today's lodging industry evolves, more and more hotels are giving the responsibility for protecting life and property to the security department. This increasingly includes risk manage-ment, or protection against contingencies that might prevent normal hotel operations and reduce profit. As more hotel execu-tives become familiar with the concept of risk management, the security function focuses less on enforcement and more on loss prevention. Such challenges indisputably require an increasingly well credentialed contemporary security manager (Fischer, pp. 20–21).

At last, the lodging industry has realized that public law enforcement resources have declined and cannot effectively control crime. The use of a professional security department, supplemented by security technology, CPTED, and security awareness among hotel staff and guests, is a viable option to prevent crime within and around a hotel.

REVIEW QUESTIONS

1. How did Pinkerton contribute to the security profession?

2. What changes need to occur for senior management to realize the importance of lodging security?

3. With public law enforcement resources decreasing, how should private security be adapting to increased responsibility?

$$2$$

Professional Organizations and Career Opportunities

INTRODUCTION

Since the late 1980s, lodging security has become a main focus in the hospitality industry. Whereas security was almost unheard of twenty or even ten years ago, there are now executive security professionals reporting directly to presidents or vice presidents of many companies, and having a major impact on management decisions made by the chain or individual hotels' general managers or managing directors. Thus, although career opportunities in the hospitality industry vary, lodging security has taken on a solid function, and this can be predicted to continue in the near future. With the current wave of emphasis on professionalism, it is an individual's training, education, and practical experience that will determine his or her career opportunities in this field.

The heightened interest in the broad-based security professional of today came through the diligent efforts of a few organizations:

- The American Hotel and Motel Association (AH&MA) Security Committee and Safety and Fire Protection Committee
- The American Society for Industrial Security (ASIS) Standing Committee on Lodging Security
- The International Lodging Safety and Security Association (ILSSA)

These organizations have helped identify the need for standards of competence and professionalism in lodging security personnel. They have devoted their attention to higher goals of education, training, and broad-based knowledge for security professionals.

Unfortunately, these areas have been deficient in the past, which resulted in the generalists' attitude and approach to this field. There is also an old myth that lodging security is characterized by transitory personnel. All these organizations, however, have had a major impact on reversing negative perceptions and attitudes and promoting a positive profession, both nationally and internationally.

The ASIS Standing Committee on Lodging Security was founded with the following vision statement:

> To aid the lodging industry by developing educational and professional programs for security personnel; advocating the use of new security management techniques; assisting in minimizing industry losses; encouraging networking and enhancing professionalism. (*Dynamics,* May/June 1994).

Committee Goals and Objectives:

1. To ensure the Lodging Security Committee is in operation by meeting ASIS Headquarters criteria

2. To act as a technical and non-technical resource to the lodging industry on issues
3. To develop proactive educational programs to improve the professionalism of lodging security personnel for whom the committee is a resource

One of the overall goals of ASIS is to assist each career security person who is willing and able to qualify as a Certified Protection Professional (CPP). The ASIS Professional Certification Board revised its education and experience requirements for all CPP examination applicants as of January 1, 1994. Applicants with 10 years of security experience who are not using education on their applications must have 7 years or 84 months of responsible charge (RC) experience (increased from 5 years or 60 months). Applicants substituting education for experience should continue to use the requirements that became effective in August 1993 (*Dynamics*, May/June 1994, p. 22):

Degree	Security Experience	RC Needed
Associate's	8 years	6 years
Bachelor's	7 years	5 years
Master's	6 years	3 years
Doctoral	5 years	3 years

The results of the increased requirements will become more evident during the next five to ten years, as employers and the public become more aware of the CPP designation.

As shown above, education and work experience are prerequisites for consideration of a candidate. If the candidate meets these criteria, he or she must take an examination on both mandatory subjects and on four out of thirteen optional subjects (e.g., lodging security). This series of tests will clearly identify the person's knowledge and capabilities. It is through this program, ASIS seminars, and courses offered by colleges and universities across the country that the highest standards of professionalism in lodging security will be achieved.

The AH&MA Security Committee's primary goal is to assist members in achieving more effective security programs. It seeks to benefit the public, guests, and employees through educational programming and security research.

The primary goal of the AH&MA Safety and Fire Protection Committee is to assist the lodging industry by working with appropriate federal, state, and local government agencies on fire protection and safety programs for guests and employees. It also provides and disseminates safety and fire protection information. The committee coordinates its activities with the National Safety Council, National Fire Protection Association, and other fire safety organizations.

The International Lodging Safety and Security Association (ILSSA) has been in existence only since January 1993. Yet it has gained considerable recognition rapidly, thanks to the publicity of security journals. Unfortunately, it has taken the lodging security profession so long to recognize the need for and solid future of such an organization that it is only now being recognized by many in the hospitality industry. The objectives behind ILSSA are simple:

- To create a medium by which all hotel security director associations can interact on issues of guest protection, employee safety, and total asset protection
- To create an internationally recognized organization to promote the professionalism of lodging safety and security directors within the security industry
- To promote educational and research opportunities specific to lodging safety and security within the hospitality industry
- To promote the creation of security standards within the hospitality industry

FACTORS INCREASING LODGING SECURITY OPPORTUNITIES

Among the factors that tend to create inviting career paths in this field, none is more significant than the explosive growth of the protection function. Other positive signs, not only for future job growth but also the potential for advancement, include the following:

- The increasing professionalism of security is reflected in higher standards of educational criteria and experience, and correspondingly higher salaries, especially at management levels.
- The rapid growth of the loss-preventive function has created a shortage of qualified personnel with management potential, meaning less competition and greater opportunities for advancement for qualified professionals.
- The shift in emphasis to programs of prevention and service, rather than control or law enforcement, has broadened the lodging security function within the hospitality industry.
- The acceleration of both two-year and four-year college degree programs in criminal justice and security management is creating a new awareness at the corporate management level of a rising generation of trained lodging security personnel. Many companies, especially the larger corporations, are actively emphasizing the degree approach in hiring.
- As in many other areas of this society, the security profession is belatedly recognizing the needs and the potential contributions of women, blacks, and other minorities. Thus, opportunities for these groups are particularly good. The greatest recent growth in the protective services has been in the employment of female security professionals.

THE LODGING SECURITY OCCUPATION

The lodging security profession has been characterized in the past by serious neglect of many security responsibilities. This attitude has only slowly been changing despite several very large awards recently granted by the courts against hotels charged with negligent security, particularly in the area of protecting guests. However, this neglect, coupled with court-mandated responsibility, has created growth in the lodging security profession.

Opportunities in the hospitality industry exist in great numbers for security professionals. The salary range, unfortunately, is relatively low in relation to the security industry as a whole. However, the entry level for a person with any combination of hotel experience, security education, or management experience can be quite high, with clear opportunities for advancement.

In the same way, the future of lodging security in high-rise hotels and in facilities with adjoining casinos, amusement parks, convention centers, malls, and the like offer great potential for the security professional, because of the growing emphasis on the family concept, which entails a facility that caters to the entire family's desired entertainment. Some potential position titles include:

> Corporate Director of Safety and Security
>
> Director of Safety and Security
>
> Security Manager
>
> Assistant Director of Safety and Security
>
> Investigator
>
> Security Supervisor
>
> Security Officer
>
> Fire/Life Safety Officer

CONCLUSION

It is important to note that both salary scales and security functions vary for a variety of reasons, even for the same type of industry. Yet it is possible to foresee lodging security's coming of age during the 1990s and early 2000s. The Rand Report reflects many of the issues mentioned in this chapter, and portrays the earlier generation of security personnel as being aged, poorly trained, and underpaid. The report notes, however, that today's security personnel are younger, better paid, and better trained than security officers at the beginning of the 1970s. They are also more likely to be women or minorities.

Still, more universally accepted standards of training are needed. Higher wage scales are needed. The opportunity for vertical movement within the security structure must be both real and perceived. Yet even in these areas there are encouraging signs, and the higher standards of professionalism promoted by the lodging security organizations will bring these goals closer.

ASSOCIATION ADDRESSES

ASIS
1655 North Fort Myer Drive
Suite 1200
Arlington, VA 22209
(703) 522-5800
Fax: (703) 243-4954

AH&MA
1201 New York Ave, NW
Washington, DC 20005-3917
(202) 289-3100
Fax: (202) 289-3199

ILSSA
P.O. Box 467
Boston, MA 02117
(617) 351-7302
Fax: (617) 424-7467
Note: ILSSA has local chapters in each major city.

REVIEW QUESTIONS

1. What factors are increasing career opportunities in lodging security?

2. Describe the organizations that contributed to the professionalism of lodging security.

3. List six of the seven potential position titles in lodging security.

Education
3

Until recently, few lodging security officers were educated beyond high school, and on-the-job training was at an all-time low. Hence, most lodging security staff had little to no training to perform the tasks so often assigned to them.

Fortunately, back in 1976, the Task Force on Private Security published its findings on the private security industry. These findings substantiated an earlier (1968) study by the Rand Corporation, showing the private security occupation as an unregulated industry. Both studies addressed the need to train security personnel and the need for academic professional preparation programs. Years later, the Hallcrest Report, presented in 1985, focused on some improvements in both areas.

In 1975, the First National Conference on Private Security met at the University of Maryland, and concluded:

> Although there is no comprehensive involvement by colleges and universities to provide educational opportunities for private security personnel, it should also be recognized

that there is little evidence that the security industry or government agencies encouraged their development (*Private Security*, p. 270).

Ever since this meeting, there has been much discussion of private security components and agencies, especially in relation to security education and training. As a result of increased interest in this area, the Law Enforcement Assistance Administration (LEAA) funded the National Task Force on Private Security to study security from all perspectives. Headed by Arthur Bilek, the task force developed a comprehensive study that went beyond the scope of the informative 1968 Rand Report. Bilek wrote in 1976 that the report of the Task Force on Private Security:

> is premised on the belief that the private security industry constitutes a massive resource that holds great promise for crime. The purpose of the report is to propose how to upgrade the ability, competence, relationships, and effectiveness of that resource for the anti-crime effort (quoted in Fischer, pp. 34–35).

This report was adamant about the need to develop standards and goals for private security. In fact, it boldly accused the industry itself of already having recognized the need to upgrade its operations. More importantly, the report stressed that "the number one need is to overcome the public's misperception that they can leave crime fighting entirely to the police." (*Private Security*, p. 18) This was a milestone and guaranty that the industry and public will receive the full benefits of the private security profession. The report heavily implies the need to improve the quality and performance of security services through training and education (ibid., pp. 1–18).

In addition, the 1980 Hallcrest Report outlined specific strategies for joint efforts by public law enforcement and private security to improve the deployment of police resources and the interface with the private security industry.

THE STATUS OF PRIVATE SECURITY TRAINING

The status of private security training has traditionally been low. A study conducted by the Private Security Advisory Council in 1978 for LEAA indicated that although security training programs were being offered by law enforcement agencies, educational institutions, training facilities, and contract or proprietary security firms, the quality varied widely. The dissimilarity in the programs was explained by the simple fact that there were no uniform standards for courses' content, length, method of presentation, instructor qualifications, or student testing. The report of the Task Force on Private Security found the same lack of quality programs and for the first time made specific recommendations. Unfortunately, many of them have yet to be implemented, although the Hallcrest Report indicated that some progress has been made.

In 1991, then-Senator Al Gore introduced Senate Bill 1258 (51), which was an attempt to introduce basic hiring standards for the security industry. This proposed legislation was later killed because of a lack of support and objections from a variety of lobbying groups, not the least of which were from the police lobby. The bill's defeat was largely the result of political infighting by vested interests. Nevertheless, it was a step in the right direction.

In 1992 Representative Martinez from California sponsored H.R. 5931 (52). Like the Gore Bill, this legislation called for minimum hiring and training requirements. Known as the Security Officers Quality Assurance Act of 1992, it was based on nine points:

- Rapid growth within the industry
- Opportunity for employing entry-level applicants
- Demand for qualified, well-trained security officers
- Wide variation in present state requirements
- Allowances needed so employers can screen applicants
- New-hire training requirements needed
- Potential improvement in public safety if appropriate screening and training were required

- Need for states to enact regulations imposing minimum standards that are the same nationwide for screening and training
- State security officer regulation (a guideline for training and experience) should apply to all security personnel whether employed by security contractors or other employers (Dalton, pp. 247–248)

Some states have adopted their own regulations through legislation. For example, the New York Security Guard Act of 1992 requires eight hours of initial pre-assignment training and forty hours of on-the-job training. California's Assembly Bill 508 (53), passed in 1993, is specific to the health-care industry. It requires hospitals to provide a security staff, train all emergency and trauma department personnel in security topics, and provide specific training to security personnel about emergency room conditions involving violence.

The Inadequacy of Private Security Training

To further stress the need for private security training, Kakalik and Wildhorn reported in 1977 that private security guards typically had no more than eight to twelve hours of training in security, that many of them had received less than two hours, and that some had received no training. Their survey indicated that 66 percent of all private security personnel had received no training before reporting to work, and only 7 percent had received more than eight hours of training before beginning their jobs. More revealing were these statistics: 19 percent were assigned to work alone on their first day and, although approximately half of all private security personnel were armed, less than 20 percent had received any firearms training (*Private Security*, pp. 35–36).

The Rand Corporation developed a test to determine the quality of private security guards' performance. The test included forty-four chances to make mistakes on the job. Twenty of these mistakes were considered to be fatal—that is, resulting in grounds for possible criminal and civil actions. The average number of mistakes was ten. More than 99 percent of the guards tested made at least one mistake, 97 percent made one fatal error, and the average number of fatal errors was 3.6. Thus, it appears that training for private security personnel is less than adequate. This may be one reason why the public law enforcement sector has such a poor opinion of the private security industry. If private security is to have the impact on crime predicted by the Task Force on Private Security, we must professionalize the occupation.

DIRECTIONS FOR INSTITUTIONS OF HIGHER EDUCATION

In November 1978, a seminar entitled "Meeting the Changing Needs of Private Security Education and Training" was held at the University of Cincinnati. It served as a follow-up to the report of the Task Force on Private Security and the First National Conference on Private Security. The majority of participants were academics.

The interest of the academic world in security education has increased recently, but it is certainly not new. The demand for improved training and education in the field of security has existed since 1957 (Fischer, p. 35). Yet questions still remain unanswered as to what roles the institutions of higher education, business, and the federal government should play in giving direction to security programs.

The federal government was very supportive of developing academic public law enforcement programs. The major impetus for this change came from the LEAA. The LEAA was also instrumental in stimulating interest in private security education by sponsoring the Task Force on Private Security. Its 1976 report suggested that private security education and training in the 1970s were at the level of public law enforcement in the 1960s. The LEAA might have taken an active role in funding educational programs, granting scholarships, or providing technical assistance, but the 1981 federal government spending cuts resulted in the elimination of the LEAA. However, since security deals primarily with private companies—as opposed to law enforcement, which is concerned with society as a whole—the question arises whether the federal government should fund such efforts. Perhaps support for educational opportunities and funding for private security should come from the private sector.

Financial support from the professional private security organizations and companies will help professionalize the private security field. Professional training takes place through college- and university-level training and education; in addition, a variety of special training courses and seminars are now being offered by a number of agencies and organizations. As noted in Chapter 2, ASIS, through its Certified Protection Professional (CPP) program, has supported the value of such education since 1978. At this time, the impact of its educational requirements for a CPP certificate has not been demonstrated. At the beginning of the program, the CPP certificate was given to those who had proven themselves to be effective lodging security professionals through experience. More recently, however, education has become a major concern for many lodging security operations.

As more and more private security managers receive their CPP credentials, the overall quality of lodging security employees will increase, since CPP-certified people will do their best to see that the lodging security occupation becomes worthy of the term *professional*. In an unpublished study conducted during 1994 and 1995, "Security Training; Cost Effective or Not?", David Bleser (a graduating student from the University of South Carolina) disclosed the following valuable information:*

- 63% of management surveyed receive less than four hours of security and safety training

---

* Bleser sampled 65 universities and 191 hotel companies; 39 universities and 31 hotel companies responded to the survey.

- 90% of respondents offer some formal training in security and safety
- 24% of universities surveyed require some sort of security and safety training for graduation
- 61% of universities surveyed offer courses that pertain directly to security and safety
- 91% of responding hotel companies agree that universities need to offer more courses on security and safety

Bleser also recommended the following:

1. The position of Security Director must be raised to an executive level position.
2. Universities need to take a hard look at their curriculum and decide how they can implement more security and safety training.
3. Managers should have a minimum of eight hours of security and safety training.

Training vs. Education

The tradition of requiring certification of professionals through training courses offered by colleges and universities is at least 100 years old in the United States. Yet, despite the success of such programs, the controversy over the value of training versus the value of education seems to persist in the lodging security occupation.

Merriam Webster's Collegiate Dictionary (p. 367) defines education as the "act or process of educating; the discipline of the mind or character through study." It defines training as the method or process of one who trains. Training refers to the act of "forming by instruction, discipline, drill; to teach so as to be fitted, qualified, proficient." Both education and training develop skill. Yet education is aimed at developing the skills of the mind, while training develops practical and manual skills and the basic knowledge that accompanies those skills. Lodging security training can be, and is being, provided by institutions of higher learning. However, adequate *training* in private security and the credentials to which it leads should not be confused with *education* and the academic degree to which it leads.

Existing Academic Programs

The 1976 Task Force on Private Security located the following:

- 49 community colleges offering at least one course in private security
- 6 community colleges offering a certificate program
- 22 community colleges offering a two-year program leading to an associate degree
- 4 four-year colleges offering a program leading to a baccalaureate degree
- 1 graduate level program

In 1981, a study by Fischer identified twenty-five institutions that offered a four-year baccalaureate degree program in private security, seven of which also offered graduate work, and one of which offered a program only at the graduate level.

Although at least twenty-six institutions of varying size and organization offer degrees in security, certain generalizations can be made about security education at the baccalaureate level. In general, programs are small, and are staffed by faculty who have more experience in public law enforcement than in security. Despite the small size of the programs, most institutions are optimistic about the future of security education. Such optimism is expressed in plans for future expansion and support for development of a Ph.D. program in security administration.

One success story of education for security professionals has been the ASIS Foundation, Inc.'s work with Webster University. Webster University has agreed to allow its existing centers to grow based on the demand created for a security program. ASIS has given each of its local chapters the responsibility to recruit 18 to 20 program participants. The program currently has approximately 250 fully employed security professionals who are part-time graduate students. According to Sandy Davidson, Director of Research and Development, "The process is slower than I would like, but it really is a significant program which is making a great contribution to the elevation of the security profession." Thirty-six semester hours are required for the master of arts, while forty-eight semester hours are required for the master of business administration. The program curriculum must include the following courses for an area concentration or emphasis in security management:

- Security Management
- Legal and Ethical Issues in Security Management
- Security Administration and Management
- Business Asset Protection
- Emergency Planning
- Information Systems Security
- Behavioral Issues
- Integrated Studies in Security Management

In addition, the student chooses elective courses. Security management courses are offered at the following locations as of this writing:

1. Albuquerque Graduate Center
   Kirtland AFB
   8500 Menaul NE
   Suite B-395
   Albuquerque, NM 87112
   (505) 292-6988
2. Chicago Area Center
   Ft. Sheridan
   570 Lake Cook Road
   Deerfield, IL 60015
   (708) 940-4556

3. San Diego Graduate Center
    Camp Pendleton
    6480 Weathers Place #104
    San Diego, CA 92121-2958
    (619) 458-9310
4. Denver Graduate Center
    Fitzsimons Army Hospital
    Aurora Park Plaza #1
    12500 E Iliff Avenue
    Suite 100
    Aurora, CO 80014
    (303) 750-6665
5. Orlando Graduate Center
    151 Wymore Road
    Suite 2000
    Altamonte Springs, FL 32714
    (407) 869-8111
6. Pope AFB
    Education Service Office
    Pope AFB, NC 28308
    (919) 436-0014
7. St. Louis Graduate Center
    8300 Big Bend, Room 238
    St. Louis, MO 63119
    (314) 968-7017
8. Bolling AFB
    114 Brookley Ave.
    Washington, DC 20332
    (202) 561-4382

MAGAZINES AND PERIODICALS

Any discipline that claims to be a profession must have its own means of distributing information. Most accomplish this through their professional publications. Security publications have changed dramatically within the last ten years, as a reflection of the growing professionalism within the field. In a *Journal of Security Administration* article, Norman Bottom notes that, ten years ago, *Industrial Security* (now *Security Management*) and *Security World* magazines were about the only publications in the security field.

The use of journals and professional magazines in the security profession was studied by Fischer in 1981 and Palmiotto and Travis in 1985 (Fischer, p. 39). Both studies indicate that *Security Management* and *Security World* continue to dominate the field, but that other publications are also being more widely read.

General Lodging Journals

Hotel & Motel Management
7500 Old Oak Blvd.
Cleveland, OH 44130
(216) 891-2750

Hotel Business
PO Box 5420
Veterans Highway
Hauppauge, NY 11788
(516) 979-7878

Periodical Literature in Lodging Security and Loss Control

Fire News National
Fire Protection Association
One Batterymarch Park
PO Box 9101
Quincy, MA 02269-9101
(617) 770-3000

Hotel/Motel Security and Safety Management
PO Box 190
Port Washington, NY 11050
(516) 883-1440

National Underwriter
505 Gest Street
Cincinnati, OH 45203
(513) 721-2140

Risk Management
205 E. 42nd Street
New York, NY 10017
(212) 286-9364

Compliance Magazine
IHS Publishing Group
PO Box 925
Libertyville, IL 60048-9862
(708) 362-8711

General Security-Related Material

CCTV Applications & Technology
15825 Shady Grove Road
Suite 130
Rockville, MD 20850
(301) 789-0048

Security Concepts
PO Box 460
4250 North State Street
Salamanca, NY 14779-9700
(716) 945-5091

Security
1350 E. Touhy Avenue
PO Box 5080
Des Plaines, IL 60018
(708) 635-8800

CONCLUSION

Security education in general, which umbrellas lodging security education, has undeniably undergone tremendous growth in the last ten years. Academic programs in security, with a few exceptions, are very young. Most were established within the last ten to fifteen years. In general, most have been reasonably successful, as the demand for college-educated security managers continues to grow. Leaders in the field, both academics and practitioners, indicate that security should seek recognition as its own distinct area of study. While some believe that the programs can find this autonomy within the criminal justice field, others believe that the field would be better off if it were integrated into colleges of business.

No matter what the view of security education and training might be, the reality is that the field is here to stay. As recent surveys indicate, more and more security managers are seeking degrees, or already possess them. In addition, training standards are being mandated by a number of states, and some companies are already recognizing the financial benefits of a trained professional staff.

REVIEW QUESTIONS

1. Define the difference between training and education.

2. What did the LEAA contribute to the promotion of security education and training?

3. How does a college degree enhance the professionalism of security professionals in the field?

Training

4

INTRODUCTION

There are some basic essentials of a security department that are absolutely critical to its success. One essential is to ensure adequate training for all employees in order to establish the necessary framework for professionalism within the department. Every security department—regardless of the lodging facility size, number of employees, or even number of security staff, for that matter—must have some form of training.

Training programs for security employees fall into two separate categories: a program for newly hired staff, and regularly scheduled training or ongoing training for staff. To develop a program for newly hired security officers, these are some important steps to follow:

- Examine the job description and analyze tasks performed by giving the officers a survey. Ask them questions about the nature of tasks performed and the amount of time spent on each task, and discuss management concerns.

All these answers are needed to develop a profile of the
actual job.

- Identify the company and department philosophy about
the role to be played by security.
- Determine the available budget.
- Decide how training is to be conducted (e.g., using in-
house staff or guest lecturers).
- Design a curriculum that addresses actual and perceived
needs and that covers the basic skills necessary to perform the job.

From a potential liability perspective, it is essential to train
all security employees before they handle calls on their own and,
further, to ensure that the training program reflects the actual
job. For effective development and implementation, the lodging
security personnel training plan needs three characteristics:

1. The program must be well rounded.
2. Training must be continuous.
3. Proper documentation of all training must be maintained.

In most facilities, training will be tailored around management concerns. Well thought-out programs will reduce the risk
of inadequate training and can be an important aspect of strategic security planning.

Inadequate training has been a major downfall of lodging
security for years. This is also an area that receives the most criticism whenever legal issues arise about an incident. Inadequate
training claims are based upon either spending an insufficient
amount of time on a topic and/or not addressing issues that will
be encountered on the job. For example, if a security officer routinely receives calls for medical assistance, it would be unreasonable not to provide some training in basic first aid.

The need for improved training is higher now than ever
because the pressure from the public (guests and patrons) has
been compounded with the recent recognition of crime rates.

Most people today in any profession are measured by the amount of education and training they have received, which qualifies them to perform their job. For lodging security professionals, both proficiency and success are based on experience and training. Keeping abreast of the current lodging security issues is another important factor.

The recommendations of the Task Force on Private Security included:

- A minimum of eight hours of formal reassignment training.
- A minimum of thirty-two hours of basic training within three months of assignment. A maximum of sixteen hours of this time can be supervised on-the-job training (*Private Security*, pp. 99–106).

The questions most asked by management are, "Why do we need this type of training?" (i.e., is it required?) and "How much is it going to cost me?" The benefits of a well-rounded training program will be measured in the security department personnel's enthusiastic attitude and performance, improved morale, and increased incentive to do quality work. One key factor to keep in mind when training personnel is that, to retain quality personnel and assist them in their career development program, the training must be continuous.

Training provides an opportunity for advancement as well as a better understanding of a required task and its importance. A fire inspection checklist, for example, ensures fire code compliance as well as confidence in one's staff. A security manager could remind his or her staff that if it hadn't been for them ensuring that an extinguisher was operational, a major disaster could have occurred (if someone wanting to use an extinguisher couldn't because it was empty).

One of the biggest fallacies made by lodging industry management is assuming that persons coming from another security field (hospital, campus, etc.) or law enforcement need not be trained. Once again, all lodging security professionals should receive training, which should only vary according to the job function of that person within the organization. For example, the person filling the position of investigator will have special training requirements that the security officer may not receive.

One critical subject usually neglected in training is documentation. Each and every course or program used should be documented in a file with a copy of the lesson plan, hand-outs, and other materials; a class roster recording who attended; a copy of the blank exam and each individual's completed exam; and a copy of the certificate issued to each person. I use the "three-part filing theory" when maintaining certificates of training. The original certificate goes to the employee, one copy is entered in the employee's human resources file, and one copy is maintained in the security training file.

SECURITY TRAINING BY POSITION

First and foremost, all lodging security personnel should receive the same initial orientation and policy handbook as every other employee. Then, when the security staff members arrive in their departments, the training program is outlined in respect to their positions.

Security Officer

The following is a partial list of training subjects that may be found in a typical security officer training manual:

1. Introduction to law
2. Tort law
3. Report writing
4. Hotel fire alarm
5. Using fire extinguishers
6. Evacuation procedures

7. Security awareness and prevention
8. Key control and guest privacy
9. Handling disturbances
10. Back care techniques
11. Health hazards in the workplace
12. First aid and CPR
13. Guest relations
14. Training for Intervention Procedures by Servers of Alcohol (TIPS)
15. Crisis prevention program
16. Hazcom
17. Bloodborne pathogens
18. Techniques of observation and patrolling
19. Two-way radio procedures
20. City and state liquor laws

Security Supervisor

The supervisor training program will obviously entail leadership courses beyond the basic ones listed for the officer:

1. City licensing regulations
2. Interaction management
3. Diversity training
4. Time management
5. Security supervisor seminar
6. Investigations
7. First responder or EMT
8. Special Police Officer license
9. Fire prevention regulations
10. Elevator regulations
11. Know your sprinkler and shut-off valve system
12. Court procedures (testifying)
13. Handcuffing techniques (if used with SPO license)

Security Manager

Security managers are responsible for planning, controlling, and organizing a department; hiring and firing personnel; and, ultimately, developing and implementing the department training program. It is only when a security manager has been given guidance by senior management regarding their philosophy of the hotel that the basic training can be developed expressing policy and procedure for that facility. It is likewise important for the training requirements to be presented in a professional manner that encourages security personnel to be cheerful, cooperative, and tolerant in their dealings within the company as employees.

There are two essential traits for a security manager: good listening skills and patience. If security managers are patient, tactful, professional, and knowledgeable, their employees will learn to respect them and will be willing to seek their assistance. When other employees can trust security, they will be more apt to cooperate in the security function that is vital to both the hotel's and the security department's success.

The security manager's attitude about training and its importance sets the climate for the department. A manager who is aggressive and structures the training program to keep the security staff moving forward and progressing upward will get support from both senior management and the security staff.

CONCLUSION

Training has proliferated in the security market of the 1990s. The lodging security professional must decide which programs benefit the facility as well as the security staff. The critical issues of today's training programs are accreditation and certification. The substance of a program may be prone to scrutinization by legal representatives. Training programs, which are needed more than ever, provide skills applicable to day-to-day operations.

REVIEW QUESTIONS

1. List five training courses a security officer should attend and why they are important to that job function.

2. What purposes does training documentation serve?

3. What is meant by the term *inadequate security training*?

5

Organizational Structure

THE CORPORATE STRUCTURE

In the past ten years, security has reached a higher corporate level. Gone are the days of security reporting to rooms managers, controllers, or building engineers. Corporate security directors now report directly to senior corporate executives. The hotel industry has even seen such positions as Vice President of Security and Vice President of Loss Prevention emerge, either in larger hotels (such as those located in Las Vegas) or at the corporate level. One key objective of any security professional at this level is to learn how to manage opportunities to increase profits company-wide, while remembering that labor, raw material, and fixed expenses cannot be reduced. Unfortunately, it is often only when security is seen as contributing to profits that the profession is seen as a legitimate business representative.

Most corporate security directors act as staff liaisons with their hotel security managers. According to Sennewald, a general description of the corporate security director's functions is as follows:

1. Establishes corporate security policies that serve as guidelines for divisional (company) security operations
2. Serves as an advisor and counselor to divisional senior management in terms of their assessment of how effectively security is functioning
3. Serves as an advisor and counselor to a security manager, giving support by way of professional expertise, advice, encouragement, and criticism
4. Serves as a central clearing-house and information center for all divisions within the corporation, disseminating important information about the industry as a whole
5. Provides for the few but important security services needed by the relatively small corporate organization comprised of, as a rule, top-ranking executives in the company (p. 21)

SECURITY DEPARTMENT ORGANIZATION AND ROLE

The structure, size, and reporting level of a security department will differ widely by hotel chain or company, due to the fact that there are presently no standards of organizational structure for certain size hotels. However, these factors will affect a department's efficiency and success within a hotel. A typical department structure consists of the security manager, assistant manager, shift supervisors, and security officers. The structure ideally coincides with the size of the property, which usually is categorized by number of rooms. Again, however, there currently is no standard.

- *Hotel with 300 rooms or less:* 2–5 staff members. A security manager is usually assigned; some hotel managers will assign security duties to front desk and engineering staff.
- *Hotel with 301 to 500 rooms:* 5–10 staff members. This size hotel has a security manager, but usually no shift supervisor positions.
- *Hotel with 501 to 800 rooms:* 10–20 staff members. Usually security consists of a manager with an assistant and supervisors.

- *Hotel with 801 to 1200 rooms:* 20–30 staff members. There is a security manager with an assistant, supervisors, and possibly an investigator.
- *Hotel with 1200+ rooms:* 30 or more staff members. Not only is there a security manager with an assistant and supervisors, but also an investigator and possibly additional specialized security persons handling other job functions such as fire/life safety, gambling fraud or monitoring, etc.

Larger hotels, such as those with 4000–5000 rooms, need to be assessed per property because of attached facilities (e.g., amusement parks, casinos, theaters).

Director of Security or Security Manager

In most hotels the department head usually will be called the director or manager. Commonly, the title "Director of Security" (or Director of Safety and Security, Director of Loss Prevention, Director of Security and Risk Management, Director of Loss Control and Security, and so on) is used to denote multiple property responsibility or multi-job function responsibility. He or she reports to a member of senior management—either an operations manager (resident manager) or directly to the managing director (general manager). A "Security Manager," on the other hand, is usually responsible for a single property, or else has the primary job function of security and reports to varied levels of management depending on the company. The older term "Security Chief" is becoming obsolete in the lodging industry.

Assistant Director of Security or Assistant Security Manager

It is very important for the department head to have an assistant who can substitute when the manager is not present and manage the department operationally on a daily basis. A security department will encounter difficulties operating effectively with just a single person in charge. There will always be some situation to which the department head cannot attend, due to the usual limitations of a regular work schedule. A hotel cannot afford to depend on the availability of a single individual. The role of the assistant security manager should be just that—to assist the director/manager by shared job tasks such as scheduling, payroll, training, hiring and firing, and coordinating department meetings. The assistant in most hotels must be capable of working flexible hours and days.

Security Supervisor

The management structure of a security department should include shift supervisors: individuals designated as being responsible for the officers working a given shift. The supervisor is the vital link between employees and security management. The supervisor represents management's needs and views to the officers and at the same time has the responsibility of representing the needs and views of the officers to management (Sennewald, p. 62).

Without a knowledgeable supervisor available, staff are left to make decisions in haphazard ways. A lack of structure could lead to an increase in poor decisions. Even if there are no actual supervisory personnel, some system of supervision must be in place. Some options that enhance control over line employees include, but are not limited to, the following:

- Unannounced spot checks on staff performance at varying times and days
- Mandatory activity reports that indicate patrols made, calls for service (opening doors, returning found property, etc.), and times these events occurred
- Security rounds using some type of audit checklist or device (such as a watchman clock or its contemporary counterpart, the wand) that records the time when the

officer made the rounds and indicates that he or she actually was at the designated checkpoints.

Security Officer

Relatively little instruction material is available concerning the individual lodging security employee's role, contribution, or importance in the overall security function. It must be remembered that regardless of how knowledgeable security management may be, the line employee's performance is the ultimate measurement of success (Sennewald, p. 65). The security officer's daily patrolling and presence have a deterrent and prevention effect that must be acknowledged. This is true both for employees and would-be criminals intending to commit a crime.

SIZE OF THE DEPARTMENT

The size of a security staff required will generally be proportional not only to the number of rooms, but also to size of the facility (expressed in terms of square footage or acreage) and the number of employees on the hotel payroll. It also will depend on a number of factors that must all be considered simultaneously. In a pre-existing hotel, it is somewhat easier to determine staffing needs by reviewing the history of problems (crime statistics) and guest-related issues addressed by security. If there are records available for review, a workload analysis can be conducted to indicate the types of calls for service and their distribution according to times and days of the week.

One rule of thumb that deserves mention concerns the number of staff required to cover a single post around the clock, for three eight-hour shifts. The number is not 3, but 4 1/2 or 5 persons, to allow for days off, vacation, sick time, training and other administrative tasks.

Other important factors to be considered include the design of the property and the location of the property relative to both the neighborhood and the type of setting. An urban hotel in a high crime district should anticipate overflow problems from the neighborhood, such as streetwalkers, vagrants, and trespassers. A hotel in a suburban location that is accessed only by motor vehicles and is surrounded by a residential community is less likely to experience the problems of the urban property. Crime rates, economic growth or decline, climate conditions, and the availability of public safety resources such as police, fire, and ambulance services must all be taken into account when planning staff size and distribution.

REPORTING LEVEL IN THE ORGANIZATION

The level in an organization to which security reports will greatly affect the ability of the department to achieve desired results. Lodging security departments have been known to report to a wide variety of managers, including the managing director, general manager, operations manager, human resources manager, building superintendent, and—perhaps most commonly—the rooms division manager. Ideally, however, the security department should report to the highest level as possible; the operations manager is practical, for example.

If the property is operated in such a way that the general manager is accessible to the security manager, then this is the person to whom security should report. A general manager's schedule is often so busy that it precludes regular accessibility except to a few senior managers. The security manager needs to be able to communicate routinely with the senior manager who oversees the security department.

There are other problems caused by having security report to middle- or lower-level managers or to a manager who represents only one area of the company's operation.

First, each layer of management that security must penetrate to reach the general manager must be acutely and accurately aware of the problems. The more layers of people a manager has to communicate through, the greater the chances of misrepresentation. Second, not everyone in an organization is an advocate for the security and prevention needs of the hotel. It is clearly possible for a middle-level manager who oversees the security department to lack the enthusiasm needed to both advocate for and utilize security successfully. Third, in order to maintain a global perspective, it is critical for the security manager to be aware individually of all aspects of the hotel's operation, including sales, accounting, human resources, and so forth.

Some security professionals lack a broad company-wide perspective on the role of security. Their narrow view does not take into consideration how the entire operation is affected by their department. Security solutions must be consistent with the overall operation of the hotel. Closing the general storeroom at night, for example, may reduce losses in inventory, but such a "loss prevention" decision will also have an adverse effect on other departments such as banquet and F & B (food and beverages) personnel who need items immediately.

QUALIFICATIONS OF SECURITY PERSONNEL

To hire quality staff, the selection of security personnel must receive 100 percent attention from the manager and/or assistant. It is essential for all security personnel to be hired directly by the security department managers and not by the human resources department. In most cases hotels will hire personnel based on their immediate need, forcing themselves to hire the next available applicant. It has been a common practice for hotels to hire retired police officers and would-be police officers who for some reason have not been accepted onto the force and so work in security. There are clear pros and cons to this approach related to hiring managers, supervisors, or officers.

The Security Manager

Many security managers are hired because they have a work history that includes experience such as law enforcement for a municipality or a federal agency. Traditional management thinking has been that this type of candidate has had extensive experience handling crime-related problems, is usually trained, and has many contacts within the police force or city/state government. For these three reasons, such a choice would seem reasonable and appropriate. Senior management must consider, however, the actual needs of their hotel. Not all properties are inundated with crime and seldom is the job of security solely focused on crime. Furthermore, it is far more cost-effective to deter crime through broad-based prevention programs than to expend resources trying to apprehend and prosecute criminals.

Another drawback frequently encountered by hiring the retired local, state, or government employee is his or her view that the lodging security job is only a second source of income and, hence, not that important. These comments are not meant to say that no former police officers or government agents can succeed as security managers, because many have, but simply to point out the problems associated with their basic orientations, lack of management skills, and, perhaps, lack of incentive.

A preferable candidate for such a position is one who is able to understand and work within a business organization. Hotels are more likely to have an emphasis on prevention, management principles, and labor issues, rather than on arrest and prosecution. Thus, a person with well-rounded management skills is far more likely to succeed than one who has a limited sense of the role of security.

Other Security Personnel

Security managers are the most important people in the security department because they set the tone of the organization by their example. However, careful selection of other security personnel should be the second-most important task for security managers filling a department. Lodging security is still a developing profession and, in some people's minds, is subordinate to police work. Consequently, many younger security officers see their positions as interim steps to becoming police officers. This is fine; working in hotel security allows them to develop experience and maturity. Although police officers currently may enjoy a better public image, they are not necessarily better paid, have better training, or have better opportunities for advancement compared to those in the lodging security industry. Still, many people do see lodging security as a path toward public law enforcement.

The problem human resources managers, or anyone else involved in the selection process, need to be sensitive to is hiring the frustrated would-be police officer who has been unsuccessful in getting a public sector job. It is one thing, for example, to hire a law enforcement or criminal justice student who wishes to gain experience. It is quite another thing to hire the individual who cannot be a police officer and must settle for the security job. The original motivation to be a police officer must be examined. Will this candidate be frustrated in the security job? Will he or she be overly anxious to make arrests, and then be a potential liability? Will this person see the job as being a second choice and not have the commitment needed? These are some of the questions and concerns that should be raised when considering applicants for security positions. As discussed in Chapter 1, security has a number of guest service functions. It is appropriate, therefore, to hire service-oriented people.

Promotions

Promoting from within is a common practice for all types of organizations. The sense that you are getting someone as a supervisor or a manager who has established a track record and who knows the company is more comforting than hiring the unknown candidate. Prior performance, consistency, quality of work product, and reputation are all factors that should be considered. Although past performance usually is a good indicator of future performance, there are some drawbacks to adhering to a strict policy of promoting from within. First, those promoted are likely to reflect the views and values of those above them, and thus this practice will maintain the same types of people throughout the organization. It may be all right to perpetuate a type of person when it is good for the company, but when the type is not as effective as needed, it could be harmful.

DISCIPLINE

The word *discipline* is derived from the Latin *discipulus* ("learning"). The word *disciple* also comes from the same root; the early Christian disciples were considered "students" of Christ. As this word origin suggests, positive and constructive discipline is training that corrects, molds, or strengthens an employee in the interest of achieving departmental and hotel goals. Punishment, which is feared and disliked by everyone, is secondary. Any punishment connected with discipline should always be a means to an end, and that end should be organizational, not personal. In other words, the effective disciplinary process condemns the act, not the employee. It says, "You're okay, but what you did is not okay."

It is also important that discipline be swift. Whatever the nature of the problem, be it simple tardiness or careless oversight, the long-range effect of coming to grips with problems immediately is better than putting off what probably will have to be faced later. The real essence and secret of constructive discipline is its preventive nature. To train, mold, and correct now reduces the need for more difficult training, molding, and correction later (Sennewald, pp. 107–108).

Discipline is a responsibility that rests squarely on the supervisor's shoulders. It cannot be passed to a higher supervisor and should not be passed to human resources. Some weak supervisors shirk their responsibility with the idea that enforcing the regulations will hurt their relations with subordinates. The supervisor who is fair and consistent in his or her treatment of employees will gain rather than lose respect through being firm and expecting conformity to the rules. Some make the mistake of believing that discipline is only directed at the inefficient worker.

All employees require constructive discipline. Most employees want to do a good job. If care is taken in giving assignments, there will be fewer failures and fewer disciplinary problems resulting from failures. However, there are six fundamental rules in the disciplinary process that have universal applicability. As presented by Sennewald, these are:

Rule #1: Put rules in writing. Make certain that employees understand the rules. No rule should be assumed. If a rule is worth having, it is worth writing down.

Rule #2: Discipline in the privacy of an office. To the employee, being corrected for deficiencies in conduct or performance is a sensitive and frequently embarrassing experience. Being corrected in the presence of others is considered degrading, and the end result of that approach is seething resentment and angry embarrassment—emotions that are counterproductive to the true disciplinary goal.

Rule #3: Be objective and consistent. Effective discipline condemns the act, not the person. This approach is obviously objective; personalities are not the issue, or at least should not be.

Rule #4: Educate, do not humiliate. The concept here is to help, not hurt an employee who has failed to meet standards of conduct or performance. If the disciplinary action truly corrects, trains, or molds the individual to meet standards, they come away from the experience with better insight into themselves and what the company expects. They come away educated.

Rule #5: Keep a file on all employee infractions. Documented incidents of past failures are a necessary and useful reference for repeated incidents.

Rule #6: Exercise discipline promptly. As time passes the infraction, whatever magnitude it may have, becomes vague and almost controversial. (pp. 110–113)

No company likes to discipline its employees or separate them from its employment. However, disciplinary action must be taken whenever an employee violates any rule of the hotel, fails to adhere to any policies and procedures, or fails to uphold the spirit of the hotel's mission. All disciplinary action should promote progress, unless the severity of it merits certain action:

- Counseling—interdepartmental counseling (i.e., consultation between department heads)
- Verbal counseling—given on first official hotel offense, placed in human resources file
- Written counseling—generally given for repeat offense after verbal counseling, placed in human resources file
- Suspension—given as a result of multiple offenses, or when a serious rule violation occurs. Usually means taking a few days off without pay
- Termination—final processing of separation from the company

SECURITY'S REPUTATION

A hotel's reputation as a safe, well-run, clean, and comfortable establishment is essential for its success. The same argument can be made for the reputation of the security department and, certainly, the hotel's reputation will depend in good measure upon the success of the security program. That program's success is tied directly to the reputation and image of the department in the opinion of the hotel's employees, its guests, and the general public.

How does one establish a good reputation for the security department and its program of prevention? To be considered capable and effective from the employees' perspective, the members of the security department and the manager, in particular, must project a positive image. Image is affected by a variety of factors, including outward appearance—grooming, demeanor and attire, personality (friendly and caring but professional at all times), consistency in treatment of employees in situations requiring security intervention, and emphasis on the positive aspect of services provided to fellow employees. It is a popular trend, for example, to eliminate the traditional security uniform and replace it with business attire. The security manager sets the tone for the organization and should maintain positive interaction with all levels of employees, never using authority as a means of exerting influence or pressure on the employees.

From the guest's point of view, image and reputation will be determined primarily by the nature of the guest's contact, if any, with security while staying at the hotel. Most guests do not have any direct contact with security, and those who do will generally have it under adverse conditions, such as a theft of property or some other negative situation. Any victim, regardless of the seriousness of the loss or inconvenience, will behave in a fairly predictable manner, frequently blaming the security officer for not doing his or her job. It is essential that security personnel recognize that the guest's response is a normal reaction to stress. Furthermore, most victims know that it is unlikely that the harm they suffered cannot be undone and, therefore, really only look to the officer for some compassion and information. Most victims simply want someone to listen to their plight, which suggests that the security officers must have developed good listening skills.

To the outside world, the public at large, the reputation of a hotel's security department will depend on all the factors cited above, and the relationship the department and its members— especially the manager—have established in the community. That community includes other hotels, the local police, the courts, the general public, visiting travelers, and criminals themselves, who have been known to have their own information system. Prostitutes, for example, know which hotels are easy to work in and which ones are not.

The security manager should make every effort to become involved in community activities related to crime and the hotel's business. As mentioned, relations with local police are extremely important, especially in times of limited staffing in police departments. Problems of crime will occasionally be so serious that police assistance will become necessary. A poor relationship with the local law enforcement authorities will impede solving such problems. Security personnel must be considered thorough and competent by the general public or the hotel security department will acquire a rent-a-cop image.

ROLE OF SECURITY

Patrolling

The most basic function for the security personnel in any hotel is to perform regular patrols of the property, both inside and outside. There are three different types of security patrolling that have been utilized in hotels for decades, yet continue to serve the needs of guests, employees, and the property in general: random routine patrol, lobby patrol, and basic rounds (also called a fire watch).

In random routine patrol, the security officer walks, or in some cases drives, around the property on a random basis to check for irregularities, suspicious circumstances, and intruders. There are two objectives achieved by this type of patrol. First, any irregularity or suspicious circumstance hopefully will be discovered before a major problem develops. For example, there may be a leaking roof, broken pipes, dark hallways or stairways, and other unsafe conditions that may cause injury to a guest or employee. The second objective is crime prevention. By patrolling in a randomized fashion, potential assailants or other wrongdoers can be detected or deterred from committing their acts. It is essential that this form of patrol not become too methodical or predictable. The officer should never patrol a site in a fixed schedule or pattern; however, it is critical to have key checkpoints throughout the patrol. For example, if the officer routinely patrols the exterior of the building at quarter past the hour, it will not take very long before a person with criminal intent discovers the pattern and uses it to predict when the officer will return. This problem may also arise if security patrols a selected location every day at a specified time. An officer may be instructed, for example, to stand by the employee entrance every afternoon at 4:00 PM until the department employees have all left for the day. Someone casually studying a hotel for obvious vulnerabilities would surely spot this pattern.

The second form of security patrol commonly employed in a hotel is lobby duty or surveillance. Any area of the hotel open to the general public (e.g., lobby, function areas, restaurants, shops) requires a different type of patrol. The officer who is assigned to a public area, such as the lobby, must stay in one general location for extended periods of time to fulfill his or her duty. There are three benefits or purposes filled by this type of security presence:

1. Observance of undesirable persons or behavior
2. Assisting guests or others
3. Deterring crime as a visible presence

Although the appearance of security will be discussed later in this text, it is important for the lobby security officer to have a high visibility unless some form of plainclothes surveillance is being conducted.

The third and most traditional form of security patrol is the fire watch. It differs from randomized patrol, although both may be accomplished simultaneously. On a fire watch, the officer patrols every floor and section of the building, including locked areas, in hopes of discovering any potential fire hazard, smoke, or actual fire. It is common practice to utilize some type of watch clock, checklists, or an electronic wand (described below) to record what items or areas were checked and at what time. Caution should be taken by security managers to control the keys and disks that are imprinted from this equipment to prevent tampering and destruction. Accurate records should be maintained with the daily log books and incident reports, mostly for insurance purposes but for legal purposes also. A contemporary version of the watch clock is an electronic device that reads bar codes similar to those used in grocery stores. The officer carries the device, which is about the size of a hand-held calculator, and passes it by a code placed on a tag at the location to be checked. At the end of the shift, the officer can insert the device into a recorder, which will read all rounds made, critical areas missed, and so on, and generate a hard copy printout. Any of these measures is helpful to enhance the level of watchfulness necessary during late night hours.

An important aspect of patrolling for all security personnel is the awareness of arson signs. Arsonists are known to use hotels as avenues for committing theft by setting fire to one location and, while everyone evacuates, stealing the guests' or hotel's property. Other arsonists like to watch people evacuate from buildings and will usually blend in with the crowd watching the scene. The typical arsonist has little concern for a facility's occupants or the firefighting personnel. Arsonists, particularly a professional "torch," will use flammable liquid in quantity. Look for liquid containers (gas cans, bottles, cartons) that may hold accelerants that can turn a small fire into a major fire in a short time. One accelerant of which most people are unaware is basic corrugated cardboard; it will burn intensely. Other items to be noted and acted upon include:

- Dynamite charges connected with primer cord
- Hydrants or sprinkler valves that have been shut down or have deliberately damaged threads to prevent hose hook-ups
- Unusual odors such as gasoline, kerosene, or fuel oil

For further information on arsonists and arsonist methods, security managers should contact their local chapter of The International Association of Arson Investigators (NFPA, pp. 14-50 to 14-55).

Security Reports

Documentation is essential to the proper operation of a security department in any environment. Reports usually generated by a hotel security department include incident reports, activity or shift reports, and safety rules violations. Well-written, typed, and accurate record keeping is very important and helpful to the future planning of the hotel in general and of security specifically. A security manager should be able to review the previous year or more of reports and identify patterns of activity that will help direct available resources in the security program. Although security reports are important as records for insurance or prosecution purposes, they should be thought of as important management tools, not locked away in a storage room or discarded. It is easier to maintain and research incident reports if they are kept chronologically. Caution should be used when storing these records; a fire file safe is recommended. Be sure to check the state statute of limitations for civil action suits and keep all records for the required time, as well as keeping records for specific pending cases until the cases are completely settled; check with your legal department.

Lost and Found

Hotels offer a wide variety of services to guests, and like most other businesses they also maintain a lost and found department. The number of found items a hotel can accumulate varies with the size of the hotel and the volume of business within the hotel. Property that is turned in to security can potentially belong to a guest, patron, employee, or someone passing by the hotel. For ethical reasons as well as ensuring that all found property is secure, all lost and found items should be turned in to the security department daily. The property should be logged in and only given to its rightful owner on request. Lost and found sheets are critical, as well as a lost and found log book tracking the property chronologically. Another log book, entitled "Returned Property," should be maintained for property mailed back to guests who have departed already and live out-of-state. This log should track not only when but "how" items were mailed (e.g., by UPS, Federal Express, c.o.d, credit card). I would recommend this policy on mailing back found property: Remember that, although it is nice to assist a previous guest when returning property, it can get costly if the hotel is paying for the shipping. If the guest checked out and left the property, the guest should pay for shipping. If for some reason the hotel is responsible for not getting the property to the guest before they departed (delayed laundry, for example), then it should be shipped at the hotel's expense.

CONCLUSION

A security manager should develop a five-year plan when considering overall security needs. Realistically, many procedures and methods will be revised as he or she develops the department. This is essential in order to fine-tune both the operational and administrative roles within the department. Remember that change is important. It ensures both continuous improvement and personal growth for all security members.

REVIEW QUESTIONS

1. Describe the five security department structures by hotel size.

2. How does a security manager determine the size of the department?

3. Why is the security department reputation so important?

6

Policy and Procedures

HOTEL EMPLOYEE MANUAL

Policy and procedure manuals and employee handbooks are essential to the consistent, productive, and efficient administration of any business. This is especially true in the lodging industry, where there are many diverse services being offered, numerous departments with different goals and responsibilities, and a myriad of problems that could arise. It is therefore recommended that in addition to a company-wide policy and procedure manual, each hotel should have its own facility manual.

Chances are that the company-wide manual covers policies and procedures that are general for the entire company. The manual may include vital, yet basic practices and procedures for each department within a hotel. This type of manual usually is used only as a guideline, while each individual facility develops its own manuals and handbook based on its geographic location. Most lodging facilities will also have a detailed manual for each department with emphasis on its operational departments, e.g. Food and Beverage, Rooms, Security, Engineering.

SECURITY DEPARTMENT MANUAL

If there is a corporate-generated security manual, it should be used as an outline for the individual facility's security manual. A separate manual specifically for the security department is an indispensable tool to give all security personnel the same information regarding the purpose, functions, and procedures carried out by the department. Security department manuals typically contain a series of policies and procedures, directives, and references to information which may be critical (or at least helpful) to security personnel. Manuals should be designed for quick reference whenever a need arises, and they also should be readily accessible. Little is accomplished when a well-written and well-designed security manual is locked up in the security manager's office after regular business hours. Ideally, every officer is given his or her own copy of the manual, and all manuals are updated as needed, generally on an annual basis.

The contents of a manual should fall into three basic categories:

1. General Information
2. Department Policies
3. Emergency Procedures

The "General Information" section often includes a description of the department's mission, organizational chart, dress code, and job descriptions for security personnel. "Department Policies" are written statements that indicate the objective of each policy and any relevant procedures the officer is expected to follow. Finally, the "Emergency Procedures" section includes detailed information on steps to be taken by security and other hotel personnel during an emergency. For example, an emergency procedure for a fire would state the responsibilities of security staff and indicate the roles expected of other nonsecurity personnel. The following is an example format:

Fire Emergency Assignment for Security Dispatcher

a. Upon noting the single point alarm indicator activation, call the following personnel separately on the radio in the following order and wait for acknowledgment before going on:

- Unit 1—security supervisor
- Unit 6—front desk assistant manager
- Unit 7—watch engineer

Manuals are, however, meant to be used only as a guideline for expected behavior during a given situation. No one has yet to write a policy, procedure, or directive that can possibly take into account all the different possible situations that could arise, as well as a definitive procedure to prevent these situations.

Constructing Policy and Procedures

Policies and procedures need to be developed for every aspect of the security operation. By using a generic outline format, you can fill in the substantive information as you develop your manual. This ensures that there is a set way to deal with specific tasks and situations—for example:

Patrolling

Routine patrols:

Check all employee areas, including locker rooms, and service areas, including kitchens. Check all bars, restaurants, and function rooms. It is important to utilize a checkpoint in all these areas.

Lobby patrols:

Maintain a visible presence in the lobby checking all doorways, escalators, retail shops, and so on.

Basic patrols:

Check all guest room floors for suspicious persons, vandals, and misguided individuals. Check all fire exits, fire exit signs, lights, pipes, guest room doors, and peepholes to ensure a safe and secure environment. Again, utilize checkpoints to your advantage to ensure that officers are inspecting areas, as well as to have legal documentation.

Not all the employees of a hotel will have access to or even be aware of the existence of the security department's operation manual. Every hotel should, however, have a general company-wide policy and procedure manual that includes a variety of essential documents. As stated at the beginning of this section, the fundamental policies and procedures of each department need to be covered in the company-wide manual. This is especially true in the area of security. Many people think security policies only involve how to patrol the premises or the methods employed when conducting an investigation. However, there are many areas that fall under the realm of security, and all hotel employees need to be aware of the appropriate steps to be taken in a multitude of situations that are likely to arise. Such situations may include the following:

- Dealing with employee theft
- Implementing emergency hotel fire evacuation procedures
- Actions to take/avoid during strikes or collective bargaining negotiations
- Guest injuries
- Sexual harassment involving employees
- Lost and found articles
- Dignitary protection
- Escorting terminated employees
- Providing first aid and CPR
- Key management
- Confidentiality procedures
- Safety deposit box procedures for cash handling

By including in the company-wide manual the essential steps to take in certain circumstances, it can be assured that proper policies will be followed, and that employees throughout the hotel will act in a similar and consistent manner.

Report Writing

Report writing is designed to inform readers as simply and clearly as possible of the facts assembled. Including all pertinent facts and using clear and effective language to express thoughts are critical to report writing.

The hotel security department is an integral part of a business. Therefore, the security manager should think and act like a business manager. This includes generating various types of reports that disclose and describe the issues, problems, and concerns encountered by the security department. Many security managers spend too much time trying to support the efforts of law enforcement and lose sight of the fact that their departments are a vital component of the hotel. By producing reports, the security department will:

- Have an accurate record of the number and types of incidents it deals with. (It may determine trends that are occurring, and it also establishes a record for the department.)
- Learn how to most efficiently allocate manpower.
- Determine areas of weakness and potential security violations.
- Ascertain which policies and procedures need modification.
- Identify new areas of concern for which there may not be a set policy.

The Importance of Accurate Report Writing: Legal Implications The security manager must ensure that all essential parts of any incident report are written down by all security personnel and that they are the facts. Names, descriptions of individuals, vehicles, buildings, surroundings, correct dates, and times are critical when attempting to reconstruct on paper what actually took place. Often a report is not written immediately after an event occurs. People who can provide answers may no longer be available for questioning. Every security person should always carry a pen and a small pocket notebook to document key facts as they arise. Names, titles, and descriptions can often be noted quickly—even during an emergency. This information can prove to be critical months later.

In his book, *Effective Report Writing for Security Personnel*, Ralph Brislin offers the following helpful hints to remember when you are reconstructing an incident from your notes in preparation for writing a report:

1. Write what happened in chronological order. What happened first, then what happened next, and next, etc. . . .
2. Be sure to include all names, positions, titles, and department numbers of all employees.
3. Include names, addresses and, if possible, telephone numbers of all nonemployees who either witnessed or were involved in the incident.
4. Explain in plain, simple English what happened. If you mention a building by its name or number, give its location as well. Remember, many people who read this report are not as familiar with directions and location as you are.
5. When you begin to write your report, constantly refer to your notes. Don't include your opinion or comments and don't editorialize. You can give your opinion or comments about the incident in person to your supervisor.
6. Don't discard your notes. Keep them until your superior advises you to discard them.
7. Write your report before you leave work. Leaving the job before your report is written gives an unfavorable impression of your security department. (pp. 72–73)

Use the six questions, who, what, where, when, why, and how, to complete any report. All reports, log books (including front desk or manager's log book), and checklists have the potential to become legal documents. Therefore, it is critical that information be recorded completely and accurately. In criminal prosecution cases against the hotel, defense counsel has absolute access to all such reports. In civil actions, insurance claims require the production of all relevant reports to defend a claim. Any type of report generated by the hotel pertinent to a claim will be considered a relevant report. Also, when a lawsuit commences, the discovery process will require the hotel to produce all documents, including reports, memos, notes, and so on. Corporate attorneys' work products and investigations done at the local attorneys' requests are not necessarily available.

The accuracy of the reports is paramount when considering the potential legal problems wrong information could pose, as well as the unprofessional image it might give the department, and ultimately the entire hotel. First, false information may lead to defamation and libel suits. Such additional charges only complicate the original suit, and increase the amount of time and money spent on the matter. Further, the torts of libel and defamation are avoidable with the accurate and factual recording of information. Second, the professional image of the security department, and in turn of the hotel, is affected by the quality of the reports produced. Sloppy and erroneous reports reflect sloppy and apathetic employees.

Professionalism means that reports are prepared prudently. It also means that reports are not merely filed away after they are generated. Professionalism dictates that reports be analyzed for content, distributed to appropriate personnel, and examined for benefits and concerns they may offer to the department. Internally, it is the senior management that reads most reports. Externally, however, attorneys and insurance company representatives read the security department's reports.

Record Retention

Depending on your state's requirements and your legal advisor's recommendations, a general time period should be established for retaining various types of records. Listed below are a few examples:

- Incident reports should be maintained for a period of five years, or for a period based on your statutory laws.
- Records relating to pending litigation should be kept until final settlement and release by legal advisor.
- Records involving minors should be maintained until a minor reaches the age of majority.
- A record of General Liability claim should be kept until final settlement and release by legal advisor; this could be 1–6 years after actual settlement.

CONCLUSION

Every security manager who takes a position in the lodging industry assumes the hotel has a security department manual. Unfortunately, this is not the case; some managers have to step into a position and start from scratch. Technically, if a department has been operating without one, the hard part is not writing the manual—it is implementing it. Why some hotel managers are *not* willing to share security manuals is beyond me. Security managers need guidance just like other managers and from whom is it better to get a manual than from another security manager? Even if a security manager has a fairly decent manual, he or she can always learn something from someone else's operation. It is unjust if hotels from the same chain do not accept this method.

REVIEW QUESTIONS

1. Describe the three basic categories of a security department manual.

2. List five situations that a security officer would likely have to respond to and for which the officer should know the appropriate steps to take.

3. What are the implications for poor report writing procedures?

7

Property Perimeter and Exterior

PHYSICAL SECURITY

Physical security is the use of numerous devices, hardware, and equipment to control access, secure property, and detect intrusion or fire. The types of hardware and technology used in hotels includes, but is not limited to, the following:

- Computer-controlled electronic guest room locks
- Closed-circuit television cameras
- Video recording equipment
- Intrusion, panic, and barrier alarms
- Fire alarms

Further, there is a variety of fencing, walls, and other barriers designed to protect the property, its contents, and its occupants. Although hotel security departments have varying degrees of involvement in the selection and installation of equipment, they all use it and are frequently responsible for monitoring and maintaining it.

The various security equipment and systems available to hotels are very useful in augmenting the efforts of the security staff. However, security managers should be cautious not to depend solely on the hardware. Effective and consistent human security practices are the key to the success of the security program in a hotel. In addition, security managers should have contingency plans in case a piece of hardware fails, someone tampers with it, or there is a temporary loss of power. As our society becomes more technologically oriented, the risk of becoming too dependent on some types of equipment increases. In a hotel, adequate security still requires a well-trained, alert, and conscientious security staff and the integration of basic security concepts into all aspects of the hotel's operation.

Perimeter

One of the most important questions for hotel security is, "Where are the hotel's property lines and how are they identified?" Yet not only is this seldom asked, but its answer is seldom known until it has become a legal issue as a result of an incident. The security manager must ensure that copies of all property surveys or blueprints are on hand. In addition, a file should be kept, including the surveys (photographs of the area that show how the property line is identified). Any and all signage, fencing, walls, pillars, or other identifiable landmarks should also be shown, in case the property line changes at some point.

The hotel's perimeter will usually be determined by its function and location. A hotel in downtown Boston would not likely be surrounded by a fence and would open directly onto the sidewalk of the city streets. However, a suburban hotel that has outdoor recreational facilities may or may not wish to have a barrier around them, such as a fence or wall. Yet if the community would have access to an area from which the hotel plans to make revenue or uses for private functions, the hotel would be likely to have a perimeter barrier.

Both natural and structural barriers can be found around hotels today. Structural barriers are permanent or temporary devices such as chain link fences, grille gates, stone walls, wood fences, cement roadblock obstacles, screening, or any other construction that will serve as a deterrent to trespassers. Natural barriers consist of topographical features used to deter or deny access. These may consist of cliffs, large stones embedded in the ground, canyons, dense growth, or any other terrain or feature that is difficult for someone to bypass. As a caution, it always must be remembered that any barrier or obstacle can be penetrated by someone determined to do so (Fischer, p. 138).

Any opening in a perimeter barrier must be viewed as a potential security threat. The most commonly used access point onto any property is the gate that allows people to drive or walk straight onto the hotel property. Most hotels do not have a gate or barrier check point because they are, after all, in the hospitality business. Other openings or barriers to be considered for perimeter security are sewers, culverts, drainpipes, utility tunnels, exhaust conduits, air intake pipes, manhole covers, coal chutes or tunnels, and sidewalk elevators (Fischer, p. 142).

Hotel Exterior

In most cases, the walls of inner city hotel buildings act as the perimeter and/or property line. If this is the case, the security manager should view the exterior of the building as a perimeter barrier. The key to surveying the exterior wall of a building is to focus on all windows and openings for potential penetration. In addition, the roof of the building should be considered for potential access points where there are skylights, exhaust vents, air conditioning units, or fire escapes. In any hotel sharing a common wall with another facility, the security department should analyze the makeup of that wall for possible penetration.

Once again, any barrier can be breached. However, if barriers are patrolled and inspected randomly, the penetration may be prevented. Most criminals will assess a hotel prior to committing a crime and decide whether it is a hard or soft target. A hard target is one that has strong barriers and security staff patrolling those barriers randomly to prevent any intrusion. In contrast, if a hotel only has glass windows as a barrier and the criminal knows the hotel is not patrolled, he or she will consider it a soft target and break into the hotel by way of the glass.

Any hotel chain that has a corporate research and development division should consider having this group work hand-in-hand with the corporate security director. The director could use the concept of crime prevention through environmental design (CPTED). This would allow for designing security measures while designing the hotels.

The CPTED concept, coined by Dr. C. Ray Jeffery in his book by the same title, expands on the assumption that "the proper design and effective use of the built environment can lead to a reduction in the fear of crime and the incidence of crime, and to an improvement in the quality of life" (Crowe, p. 1). This translates to many practical and useful applications. Author Timothy Crowe, in his book *Crime Prevention Through Environmental Design*, states:

> CPTED will alter and expand the security professional's perception of the immediate physical environment. Altering the perception of the physical environment increases the capacity to understand the direct relationship of the environment to human behavior and to crime. An increase in this basic understanding should result in the increased likelihood of the individual's confidently questioning or challenging decisions that affect her immediate environment—particularly those that may have a direct bearing on the safety of the individual, their family, neighborhood, or place of business (Crowe, p. 5).

An objective study of any law enforcement or security operation will reveal that the primary requirement for crime-related services is prevention, in its broadest sense. Crowe recommends that each of us ask the following three questions before we continue in our present activities, or allow our organizations to proceed within a limited understanding of the role of crime prevention:

1. What is the requirement for our services?
2. How do we spend our time and resources?
3. What are the results? (p. 18)

The National Crime Prevention Institute has adopted the following definition: "Crime prevention is the anticipation, recognition and appraisal of crime risk and the initiation of some action to remove or reduce it (the risk)" (Crowe, p. 23). Yet Crowe states that loss prevention is broader than crime prevention because it includes a wider range of behavior than what is defined legally as criminal. Loss may be defined as the removal or taking of an object or asset of value. Loss may result from poor productivity, incompetence, inefficiency, lack of motivation to complete a work task or to use resources properly, or lack of management attention. The loss of value may be financially measured, or it may be assessed in emotional terms. The improper use and management of talent also may become a loss category. Loss occurs on a broader scale through natural causes, such as storms or earthquakes (Crowe, p. 24).

Does it take a lot of expertise to understand the relationship among the environment, the roles of noncriminal justice agencies, and crime? The answer is simple. All it takes is an awareness that there is a relationship between the things that people do naturally and the amount of surveillance and access control that exists. Both offenders and ordinary people recognize the environmental cues that say, "This is a safe place" or "This is an unsafe place." Experts and sophisticated technology are not required to figure out what is going on and to take advantage of natural opportunities to make a community safer. All that is required is good sense (Crowe, p. 27).

There are two major areas for which most hotels lack the correct security priority: parking lots and exterior lighting. Most hotels will have open parking lot areas (where employees and guests park their own vehicles) and some hotels will have garage-type areas (which may have self-parking or valet parking). The location of these lots in relation to the hotel entrances and exits is critical to both guests and employees.

Parking lots should be patrolled, well lighted, and, if possible, kept under constant surveillance. A lot close to the hotel will mean less travel time for someone to go from his or her vehicle to the hotel. The location of the lot may also create a higher frequency of staff and other persons going through the lot. This may prevent criminals from wanting to act in the lot, due to the high probability of being seen and perhaps apprehended. The risk analysis conducted by the security manager (see Chapter 9, Risk Management) is an important tool to help reduce the probability of crime.

Proper posting of signs giving directions to the hotel entrance is critical. In addition, "no trespassing or solicitation" signage is vital to deter criminals and assist the hotel in the event that criminals are apprehended committing a crime on hotel property. Signs can also act as a way of forewarning someone either to do something or not to do something. They can be used as a defense in a criminal case as well as a civil case, if needed. Usually the lack of signage will be more detrimental to the hotel than having signage.

Lighting

Lighting acts as a tool for patrolling the parking lots and the perimeter/exterior of the building. The origins of lighting for security are in Paris, the "city of lights."

Louis XIV was the king of France (1643–1715). Louis introduced what would later be called urban renewal to the streets of Paris. He installed broad boulevards and extensive landscaping. Louis was proud of his beautification efforts, until he found them defaced by vandals during his morning rides. So he embarked on a massive security program that culminated in the installation of nearly 7,000 street lamps from 1700 to 1701. This was the first widescale use of outdoor lighting in history. But this lighting was installed primarily to protect *property*. In the 1700s, ordinary people got up when the sun came up and went to bed when the sun went down. People were afraid of night air, thinking that this air carried more diseases. They closed up their homes at night, even in hot weather.

Contemporary outdoor lighting, on the other hand, is viewed popularly as a fundamental device for protecting *people*. Louis XIV's lighting initiative may have changed the course of human history. The widespread confidence in the technology of outdoor lighting seems to have planted the seeds of changes that have irreversibly affected the quality of life. People now go out at night. They go to church and to school at night. They go to athletic events at night and they play golf at driving ranges that are open all night. People jog at night for convenience and comfort. People prefer nighttime for many outdoor functions.

Technology and the willingness to use it, even for Louis XIV's somewhat selfish and costly reasons, have significantly changed the course of human history. Yet most people take the presence of light for granted. Lighting engineers have learned a lot about the effects of light on human behavior. Indoor lighting, for example, traditionally was designed to provide a balance of natural and manmade lighting at the floor level. Lighting sources were placed in hallways and foyers at the center of ceilings, so that the cones of light would cover the floor. But people's eyes are not on the floor; their feet are there. New experiments have demonstrated that traditional interior lighting may not have taken advantage of its potential effects on human behavior. People stand and see at a range of 4'8" to 6'0". Accordingly, it has been noticed that people will walk near the middle of centrally lighted corridors. They will stand near the middle of centrally lighted foyers. The closer people stand to each other, the more likely they are to exhibit avoidance behaviors out of politeness and discomfort. When the light source is oriented toward the walls in hallways and foyers, people will walk or stand closer to the wall. They are more likely to establish eye contact with others because of the increased distance. They are more likely to feel comfortable and safer. Recent research also has demonstrated that there is a 30 percent reduction of noise in these well-lighted hallways and foyers.

Lighting clearly has an impact on people's perception of distance. People need distance to feel safe from potential threats. The perception of distance is important, perhaps more important than true distance. The easiest way of fully understanding this concept is to spend part of a day in an elevator. The fewer the people, the farther apart they will stand. They are more likely, however, to establish eye contact. As the elevator becomes more crowded, people will give each other social distance by practicing avoidance behaviors. They will look up or down, but avoid eye contact, even though they are touching others due to crowding. Touching is legitimate and nonthreatening when there is a crowd. However, watch what happens as the crowd departs the elevator: continued touching will be perceived as a threat, and may produce enough fear to be considered an assault.

Finally, lighting experts are thinking more than ever about how to use lighting to achieve behavioral effects (Crowe, pp. 70–71). Depending on the layout of a hotel and its outside grounds, lighting needs to be part of the risk analysis survey and determined on the basis of an individual property. The exact amount of lighting needed for a specific property can only be determined through planning. Yet some install lighting and a year later decide they need more. It is common knowledge that more lighting allows people to feel safer, and that it deters criminals from wanting to commit crimes for fear of being seen and recognized.

All lighting must be reliable and designed with overlapping illumination to avoid creating unprotected areas if individual lights fail. Back-up power supply is also necessary in case of power failure. Portable lights should be readily available for security staff when needed for special or emergency situations (Fischer, p. 146).

When planning for lighting, the security manager should keep in mind that no one type of lighting is applicable to every need. The lights most commonly used are either incandescent (common light bulbs), gaseous discharge (mercury vapor lamps that give off a bluish cast), or quartz lamps (bright white lights usually used at very high wattage). It should be the responsibility of security to be aware of their light conditions when patrolling the hotel exterior. A checklist can be developed or there can be a daily mention in the log that all lights are in working condition. If there is a problem it should be noted. Follow through to ensure that all lights are repaired immediately.

Finally, the security manager may wish to obtain a copy of the IES standards that cover lighting illumination. This has proven to be a valuable tool when conducting security surveys, to ensure the current status meets the recommendations.

Interior and Object Security

One critical step in physical security planning is to minimize or control access to a building's interior. Yet most hotels have an open-door policy, welcoming people into the hotel. The actual access control in a hotel environment generally comprises doors leading to employee areas, guest floors (elevators), and private function areas. The most common problem security faces is to control the human traffic without interfering with the function of the business operation. When conducting a risk analysis of these access control areas or check points, the security manager needs to protect against the internal thief as well as the criminal element. Doors leading to employee/office areas should be appropriately marked with "authorized personnel only" signs.

Doors and Windows

All windows and glass walls should be considered a weak point from a physical security perspective. Both the glass and the window frame need to be assessed for vulnerability. The two types of glass with which security managers need to be familiar are tempered glass (designed to protect people from the danger of flying shards) and UL-listed burglary-resistant glass (referred to as "safety-glass," it resists heat, flame, cold, ice picks, and most other paraphernalia).

Doors must be analyzed for their function. Different types of doors leading into a hotel should be used based on the amount of traffic through them, and whether each is used more as an entrance or an exit. There are four areas to be scrutinized:

1. *Frame.* Does its structure (i.e., steel, wood, etc.) meet the needs of the area being protected?
2. *Hinges.* Does it have surface-mounted hinges with screws or pins exposed that can be removed?
3. *Door.* Should it be made of glass, panel wood, solid wood, metal, or other materials?
4. *Lock.* Is the type of lock set appropriate for the area being protected?

Key Control   Key control is an essential arm of access control. Management and the security manager must assume direct control of all key systems within a hotel. Many hotels make the mistake of allowing engineering, the rooms division, and even human resources to control the key system. This should not be allowed by senior management. Key control should not be based on status or executive position.

All keys should be issued and recorded through either a computer or a card system. Keys used by employees other than managerial staff should be signed out on a daily basis. Key storage always should be maintained by security and inventoried at least three times daily. Follow up immediately on keys that are unaccounted for, even if you have to contact staff at home. If it is determined that a key is lost, rekeying should begin at once. A strict key control policy also must be in place to ensure full compliance; a set of key misuse disciplinary action steps should be outlined. The most important guideline for disciplinary action involving keys is that it should be enforced equitably for both management and nonmanagement.

The key system should be kept simple and include a change key, submaster keys, master keys, and grand master keys:

1. The *change key* is a key to a single lock within a master-keyed system.
2. The *submaster key* is a key that will open all locks within a particular area or grouping in a given facility.
3. Where two or more submaster systems exist, a *master key* system is established. This key would open any of the systems.
4. The *grand master key* is a key that will open everything in a system involving two or more master key groups (Fischer, p. 169).

Rekeying   In any size hotel, rekeying is a tedious task and probably expensive. Compartmentalization of areas by submasters usually will prevent having to rekey the entire hotel. The security manager can prevent nightmares by ensuring that very few grand master keys are issued and that these keys are accounted for when staff leave the hotel.

Many of the larger hotels, and even some smaller ones, have converted to the electronic key card systems. These systems have been around for many years and continue to be updated technologically each year. In fact, no less than three major hotel chains have mandated that their hotels be equipped with an electronic key card system within the next few years. As many know, technology is an excellent tool from an operational standpoint. However, it should never be utilized if it will compromise the safety and security of a facility and its occupants.

Author Stephen Rogers, in *Access for Success*, notes some issues security managers should consider when researching which electronic key card system is best for their hotels. As Rogers states, "Success or failure cannot be predicted unless access control needs are well thought out" (p. 22). Success in access control means not having to start over once a system has been installed. It means knowing the level of security needed and how the system will be used. Proper preparation brings the results an organization seeks in an access control system today and tomorrow.

When it comes to improving security, an organization must rank the features it needs. Reliability, degree of security, user acceptance, reporting level, and cost often top the list. Departments often rank these features differently, and a company must be aware of various departments' needs and keep track of them as they change. The least an organization should expect from an installed system is that it keep out unauthorized personnel but let in authorized users. The system should give users a fast response with little bother. It should operate reliably at all access points while supplying the needed information for effective management. Its cards, tokens, or electronic keys should be nearly impossible to counterfeit to provide the highest level of security. In addition, the system should fit within the organization's budget and should be flexible enough to prove a sound investment for many years to come.

Thus, before it begins to configure an access control system, an organization should paint an accurate picture of itself and its security needs. It should also establish an idea of what it expects its security needs will be in the future. At the forefront of decision makers' minds should be a series of questions (about access control points, CCTV positions, communications, EDP, etc.) to help them determine these needs and choose wisely from available technologies without sacrificing the quality of security (*Security Management*, p. 14A).

One of the most challenging projects on which a security manager will work is the negotiation of a lock purchase and installation agreement. Most chain hotels will have a corporate contract the security manager can use. However, if one is not available, consider the following outline:

1. Name the parties involved (i.e., company and contractor).
2. List sale and installation obligations.
3. Designate the total number of locks, their type, the exact description of lock hardware and attached accessories, the minimum criteria of lock mechanism, and acceptable standards.

4. Specify installation details: the schedule, who will perform what and when, who will provide what tools and equipment or services, and any restrictions and limitations.

5. Create a payment plan. The initial installment is paid when agreement is signed (usually one-fourth to one-third); final settlement is paid only upon successful and satisfactory complete installation. Complete a final punchlist (i.e., a checklist for all parts installed) for each device to ensure full compliance of work.

6. Plan pre-installation. All departments (engineering, front office, housekeeping, etc.) must work in conjunction with security to ensure a smooth transition and installation.

7. Establish who will attend training, who will do the training and where, who will pay for the cost of training, and what the length of training will be.

8. Give details of warranties. What is the life of the lock, its components, and all electronic devices? Do fire ratings satisfy all UL/NFPA/ANSI/ASTM standards?

9. Address agreements on replacement parts: initial stock above inventory, ordering process, turn-around time for parts, manuals to install parts.

10. Specify insurance for general liability and workers' compensation certificates.

11. Have your legal counsel review all contracts and ensure that the indemnifications meet the needs of the hotel.

12. Define labor agreement: designate union or nonunion, subcontractors, third-party involvement in hotel, guidelines for workers, and what will happen to old locks and equipment (Will locks be purchased by contractor? Will old locks be boxed and shipped at their cost? etc.).

13. Make sure to consult with an EDP representative to ensure that software will meet every need you can imagine at the time of installation and any future need. The warranty is usually different for software, so you need to

read fine print, including any coverage for programming corrections or add-ons (for example, if a suite with
connecting doors is added).
14. Specify all defaults in case of failure to provide service
or financial hardships.
15. Name exceptions. Consider natural disasters that may
cause delays.
16. Designate how notice should be given for any changes
in plans, orders, etc.
17. List references of all installations.
18. Ensure that signatures of authorized representatives are
at the end of the contract.

Access Control for Guest Rooms

The hotel has an affirmative duty, stemming from a guest's right
of privacy and peaceful possession, not to allow unregistered
and unauthorized third parties to gain access to its guest rooms.
Generally speaking, when a hotel guest has paid for a room, the
guest is entitled to constitutional protection against unreasonable search and seizure. The hotel management would normally
have no authority to permit the search of the guest's room without a search warrant, because this would violate the hotel
guest's right to privacy.

CCTV for Surveillance

There are two types of surveillance available to security when
using CCTV. The first is *overt surveillance*, which is the act of
watching someone or something from an open and obvious
point to determine and document the extent of activity. This type
of surveillance is commonly used as a deterrent to shoplifters
and patrons who might have "sticky fingers" as well as to discourage employee theft or fraud. The other kind is *covert surveillance*, the act of watching someone or something from a hidden
or unknown position to determine and document the extent of
activity. This documentation may serve as the basis on which a

suspect is apprehended for criminal wrongdoing or discharged from employment for illegal activity. Placing a camera in an unknown location gives the employee or patron no reason to change their regular illegal activities.

Object Security

Although object security comprises many additional aspects, two of them merit special mention. The first is that of securing art fixtures within a hotel. When conducting the risk analysis, the security manager should calculate the cost of art assets and then determine the best way to protect them without devaluing them in any way. Analyze what the investigation would cost if each object was stolen, replacement cost if even an option, and lost income if it was a rare object that generated hotel revenue.

The second area of concern is securing file safes, vaults, banks, and guest room safes. These are object security containers that will help the security manager deter criminals from even being tempted to steal from the hotel. File safes are crucial for all important data and information of the hotel—for example, sales records, patented materials, incident reports, human resources personnel records, payroll records, and even EDP data from nightly back-ups. Guest room safes and safe deposit boxes should be made available to guests at no charge to assure them of the hotel management's wish to provide a safe and secure environment for their belongings. Room safes allow guests to store their personal belongings without having to travel to the front desk every time they wish to deposit or retrieve something. Finally, employee banks (storage boxes in the vault that hold money for employees) should be controlled by the accounting department and audited by both the accounting department and security randomly at least on a monthly basis.

CONCLUSION

The topic of physical security alone has been the subject for many books. However, very few hotels today could survive without using some form of physical security measures. It is imperative that security managers keep up with the new technology for application in the hotel industry. The technology will change very rapidly in the next few years, more so than we can imagine today.

REVIEW QUESTIONS

1. Describe the difference between natural and structural barriers.

2. What does the term *CPTED* stand for and why is it important?

3. Describe key control and list the formats for a key system.

Internal and External Risk

8

THEFT

Theft occurs in a variety of forms, representing the single greatest challenge for security in the lodging industry. Almost all the items found in a hotel which are used by the guest (e.g., towels, pillows, phones, television, hairdryer) can also be used at home. Guests usually travel with cash, credit cards, jewelry, cameras, and other valuables that may be appealing to a thief. Large urban hotels employ several hundred employees, because the lodging industry is a labor-intensive business. Yet at the same time it creates ample opportunity for a thief to steal the employees' personal property, guests' property, and hotel property. Each of these types of burglary requires a different response or prevention measure by security. All are forms of theft and, as such, should be major concerns.

Hotel Property

Contrary to common belief, hotels generally do not "build-in" a certain dollar amount in their budget for anticipated losses. Losses are not acceptable, nor are they part of the operating costs of a business to be offset by increased room rates. However, certain types of losses are tolerated to some extent due to the sensitive nature of the circumstances surrounding the theft. An example of such a sensitive problem is the theft of a terry cloth robe and other items from a guest room by the guest. Hotel managers are often reluctant to question a guest suspected of removing towels or other objects. The risk of liability for slander and/or ill will that affects future business usually is seen as far outweighing the benefit of recovering the items believed to have been stolen.

The security manager's first task is to assess the hotel's assets, determine which of these assets are vulnerable to theft, and then devise a program that will reduce the risk. One helpful tool is to instruct the human resources department, while conducting employee exit interviews, to ask questions regarding employee theft, use of drugs, and so on. This technique usually will assist you with information to narrow down areas needing further investigation. However, the usual approach is to conduct a risk analysis (potential for loss; see details in Chapter 9, Risk Management) of the property and its assets. This entails identifying the risk of loss and determining what measures may be employed to reduce or eliminate that risk. In addition to the actual physical survey, the security manager should review all reports of loss for the previous year to assess where and possibly how items were stolen. This approach will help identify the most vulnerable areas of the hotel. Continue to conduct this survey as often as possible. This is done annually in most hotels; however, conducting a quarterly or even monthly survey would lead to the best results.

The key to protecting assets is to obtain cooperation and assistance from all hotel employees. Security managers who think they can do the job by themselves are making a dreadful mistake. Security is everyone's job! In fact, this slogan should be emphasized during an employee's initial orientation program as well as in monthly departmental meetings. Successful prevention measures depend on a well-designed program that involves input from all employees.

The security manager can work with employees in a variety of ways. First, he or she should educate employees about the seriousness of theft and how it affects them. Second, she or he should attempt to develop employees' understanding of the problem in terms that they as members of the organization can relate to and appreciate. For example, if it is made clear that all losses cut into the profitability of the property and that reduced profits, if severe enough, may result in lower wages or even laying off employees, the employees may realize that they too have a financial stake in the prevention of losses. Third, assistance from employees may be elicited by encouraging them to call and report suspicious people or circumstances and at least make an extra effort to secure valuables when leaving a work area (for example, securing tools in storage rooms). Fourth, it is essential that the security department maintain a good working relationship with all employees, avoiding morale problems created by poor communications and a lack of understanding. Employees suffering from poor morale are not going to be very concerned about protecting the assets of the employer. Finally, the security manager must work with all other department managers to get their input on solutions to the problem of losses. Some security personnel may think that the solution to the loss problem is locking up and limiting access to the hotel's assets, but if a measure interferes with the normal operation of a hotel, it will be resisted and is a guaranteed failure. In fact, the security function will be viewed as less effective unless the solution recommended includes input from the departments affected by it.

Program design is only half of the crime prevention task. The other half, which is equally important, is continuous improvement. The security manager should repeat the risk survey at least quarterly, if possible, to ensure compliance with the program, and to discover any changes in the physical structure or the hotel operation that may negate the original plan. The program must always remain flexible to meet the needs of the business. New and better methods should always be sought for improved preventive measures. When losses do occur, as they will, evaluate the loss and adjust the program accordingly.

Guest Property

One reason why hotel managers are concerned about the theft of guest property is the potential impact on future business. As will be discussed in Chapter 12, Legal Issues, most states have limited an innkeeper's liability to a fixed amount and generally that amount is not very high. A history of serious guest losses may, however, drastically affect the hotel's reputation and may also be indicative of other weaknesses in the security program which could lead to more serious crimes. For example, if poor key control were to blame for a number of guest losses, it also could increase the chances of a more serious crime such as an assault of a guest. Such criminal activity is common grounds for lawsuits against hotels.

Investigation of such losses should include, first, an examination of the locking hardware on the room to ensure that it is working properly. This could be a problem because guests frequently may not close their door tightly when leaving or when running down the hall for ice or soda. Second, determine which employees have access to the room under investigation and note them for further follow-up. If good records are kept, after a short while the same employee's name will begin to appear regularly. Once that is discovered, the investigation could focus more on that individual. Third, find out when the locks were last changed or rekeyed. There may be an overall problem with key control. Finally, check for missing room or master keys that anyone could use to gain access to guest rooms.

Prevention of guest room theft depends primarily on employee and guest cooperation. Employee cooperation and assistance were discussed above and apply to guest losses as well. Guest cooperation is more difficult to obtain because of guests' transient nature, but can be achieved to a reasonable extent. The type of cooperation sought is generally limited to two areas: use of existing risk-reducing equipment such as safe deposit boxes and in-room safes, and making sure guests close and properly lock their room doors either when they leave or go to sleep. Some hotels put small signs or fliers in guest rooms advertising the availability of safe deposit boxes and in-room safes, as well as directions on how to properly secure the door. Other hotels use the cable system on the room television to promote safety and security measures.

Employee Property

An employee's personal property, uniforms, and hotel equipment are subject to theft in locker rooms and work areas. Although the theft of such property is not generally seen as a liability problem, it should be of concern from the standpoint of employee morale. It is a well-known fact that poor employee morale will reduce productivity and will fail to promote the kind of cooperation needed by the security department to prevent other losses. The theft of any employee valuable should be treated with the same level of concern and priority as any other loss.

The two most common areas for losses to occur are locker rooms and office areas. In locker rooms, the lockers must be equipped with adequate locks and a sound key control system. (Combination lockers with one master key maintained by security work well in case of a forgotten combination or if the need arises for a locker search.) Security also should check locker rooms frequently during their patrols. This should be done randomly whenever security personnel are in the immediate area or intentionally as part of the routine patrol. When time permits, each locker should be checked to ensure it is secured, in addition to seeing that it has regular maintenance and bringing problems of abuse to the security manager's attention. (In some areas it has also been common to put push-button locks on the locker room entrance door to ensure added safety and security to those employees changing in the locker room.) Such inspections also reveal health problems (e.g., pest control) and problems such as stockpiling of uniforms or other hotel equipment (banquet utensils, housekeeping amenities, etc.).

Consistent with this approach is the need for a hotel policy on what may be kept in employees' lockers and the hotel's right to search them periodically (a two-person integrity search is recommended). In office areas, the most frequent loss occurs when employees leave their handbags, wallets, backpacks, briefcases, or gym bags unattended in unlocked desk drawers or on top of desks. The security manager needs to be sure that desks can be locked, and encourage employees to use those locks to protect their personal property.

Another common practice is for employees to leave an office door wide open to give a false impression that they are still working, when in fact they have left for the day. Yet in doing this, they may leave their personal effects in plain view for anyone to take easily.

Investigations

Any time someone is injured in the hotel or property is lost, security should conduct some form of an investigation. There are at least three advantages of a thorough investigation. First, the root cause of the problem hopefully will be discovered. If, for example, a guest became injured as a result of falling down a stairway, it is important to investigate the root cause of the fall. In such a case, the fall could be caused by torn or worn carpeting, poor lighting, lack of handrails (check diameter to ensure bar is in compliance with ADA), wet or slippery surfaces, or some factor inherent to the guest. Some possible reasons for the guest to fall include intoxication (liquor liability will be discussed later), improper footwear, bifocals, or other mobility problems. The same issues are present when an employee is injured on the job.

The second reason for a thorough investigation is prevention. By analyzing the cause of a theft, for example, security can determine how the article was stolen and then develop preventive measures to avoid similar losses in the future. The theft of food from kitchen storage areas is common to hotels and restaurants of all sizes. If investigation of this indicates that methods of inventory control are deficient, recommendations can be generated to implement better control and reduce further losses. The security manager who analyzes all incidents and implements proactive procedures will prevent incidents of theft. However, employees are constantly developing new methods to steal which, when discovered, should be used as learning tools for security. New methods of theft are usually brought into a facility by a new employee who introduces that method to other employees.

The third benefit gained from an investigation also is related to future loss prevention. In a case of stolen property or drug dealing, for example, the simple process of questioning witnesses and suspects will create a deterrent to future crime. Routinely interviewing potential suspects will help establish an atmosphere of nontolerance for crime. Employees who may be guilty of wrongdoing, or who may have considered it, hopefully will be deterred from future activity if the impression is given that the hotel management will not tolerate misconduct. A timely and thorough investigation of every incident, requiring more than just an initial incident report, will enhance the department's image and will help develop an effective security program.

Arrests and Prosecution of Offenders

Chasing suspects, making arrests, and testifying in court are also job responsibilities of a hotel's security staff. For many hotels, though, these activities often are ones of last resort when attempting to address the problem of crime and its associated losses.

Although arrests may not be the preferred option of many hotels, they may be necessary and will occur in even the safest properties. Security managers, therefore, need to be prepared to deal with the problems generated by making arrests and prosecuting offenders. If the hotel security staff will use special police powers or licenses, it is essential that they receive at least minimal training in arrest, use of force, and civil and criminal law—including the limits of their authority, use of weapons, and the rights of the accused.

In addition to training, security personnel need directions in the form of written policies and procedures. It is important to review the laws of the jurisdiction where the hotel is located to determine what restrictions may exist. For example, a state may limit the time that someone can be detained by a security officer. Most states will extend arrest authority of security officers who have been licensed as special police or deputized police to include offenses for which an unlicensed officer may not arrest, e.g., shoplifting. An arrest made without legal authority is invalid and likely to subject the officer and the hotel to civil liability. If handcuffs or weapons are authorized, additional training and policies will help ensure that proper practices are followed.

A track record of successful arrests and convictions can enhance the security program in the hotel. However, improper arrests, mishandled suspects, and unprepared testimony surely will result in acquittals and lawsuits. Juveniles need to be handled differently in some states, so check the laws on detainment and arrests.

CONCLUSION

It is critical to prevent both internal and external theft if a hotel is to survive. Many companies that include hotels go out of business due to employee theft and/or guest theft. In fact, a city or town that feels that a hotel cannot protect its employees or guests and their belongings may choose to fine the hotel or suspend its license. Thorough investigations are necessary if a hotel security manager wants to prevent future loss from theft. Finally, most hotels will have a corporate policy covering arrests and prosecution. Any hotel manager unsure of these procedures should consult the hotel's corporate or local legal advisor.

REVIEW QUESTIONS

1. Describe what procedures should be taken if hotel property is stolen.

2. Why is employee property just as important as hotel or guest property?

3. How does a security manager prepare to deal with arrests and prosecution?

9

Risk Management

INTRODUCTION

Most contemporary lodging security managers are being asked to perform risk management duties and need to know how to recognize the property risks as well as how to manage them. The idea of merging an insurance program and its risk management tools with a safety and security department is being promoted because of downsizing and economically difficult times. The actual concept of "Risk Management" presents a sensible approach to this arena; it also allows risks to be handled in a logical and systematic manner. Basically, insurance, in and of itself, is no longer able to meet the safety and security challenges faced by hotels today.

One of the first tasks a security manager must undertake is to conduct a risk analysis to recognize threats to the hotel. Because each hotel has many assets including the land, building, and fixtures, it must ensure that money is budgeted for the unexpected. Risks to property, for example, generally are overlooked; most hotels focus only on fixtures.

Risk is a relative thing and a matter of perception. It changes wildly, depending on circumstances. A satisfying definition of risk remains evasive, but its characteristics are well known. The individual who faces risk can minimize or maximize it, prioritize or deprioritize it, depending on the needs of the moment. An individual can quantify risk and transfer it to another. Security managers must learn to manipulate risk in their favor, as they do with any other business commodity. Since the 1980s, "risk management" has become one of the most widely used terms in business. And as its use widens, its meaning does, too (Walsh, p. 2).

Dr. Grose encourages risk managers to redefine risk as all "potentials" that could lead to loss. He defines nine categories or subsets that constitute risk: occupational health (disease), public relations (falsehood), safety (hazard), security (threat), quality assurance (defect), environmental control (toxicity), legal counsel (liability), human resources (discord), and loss financing (insolvency) (*Risk Management*, p. 64).

A good risk management program is essential for hotels and should include this list of minimum steps:

1. Identify risks or specific vulnerabilities.
2. Analyze and study risks, including the likelihood of an event and its degree of danger.
3. Optimize risk management alternatives:
   a. *Risk avoidance.* Remove a problem by eliminating the risk.
   b. *Risk reduction.* Decrease the potential ill-effects of safety and security problems.
   c. *Risk spreading.* Decentralize a procedure or operation so that a safety and security problem will not cause complete loss.
   d. *Risk transfer.* Remove the risk by paying for insurance coverage.

e. *Self-assumption of risk.* Plan for an eventual loss with-out benefit of insurance.

f. Any combination of the above.

4. Conduct an ongoing study of safety and security pro-grams. (This must be a total approach; there can be no shortcuts.)

Threat Assessment

Once again, the first step in risk analysis is identifying threats and vulnerabilities. Many threats to hotels are important to secu-rity, but some are more self-evident than others. It is critical to consider the specific vulnerabilities in a given situation. Each hotel has its own unique problems and threats. For example, a hotel that has paver blocks installed on top of its high-rise build-ing should be able to withstand a windstorm much better than a hotel that doesn't have paver blocks.

Specific threats are not always obvious. Although it seems to be common sense to check doors, locks, and gates to control access, accessibility through walls made with inferior materials or through a poorly constructed door or door frame is a less obvious consideration. Awareness of all the possibilities makes a good security manager. When conducting a risk analysis you should consider destruction of property by natural incidents and from a criminal mind-set to think of prevention measures. Once completed, a vulnerability analysis—also called a *security survey* or *security audit*—should be repeated at least annually.

Probability

Once the task of identifying vulnerabilities has been completed, it is essential to determine the probability of loss. For example, suppose that one vulnerability involves the theft of guest credit cards. Within the timespan that the card was stolen and then used, what measures did the hotel staff undertake? Should security expend personnel time reviewing the process to help prevent future loss? Basically, probability is a mathematical statement about the possibility of an event. The only way to prevent this type of incident is to improve procedures, which may require the implementation of physical security devices. (Note: Consult with legal counsel on the timing of any changes involving privacy of guests or state regulations.)

Criticality

Hopefully, a security manager can identify a problem area prior to when an incident occurs. To help separate the vulnerabilities into specific categories, the security manager should use the principle of criticality. *Criticality* has been defined as the impact of a loss measured in dollars. This concept must also be explored from the point that it includes area, practice, or whatever is critical to the existence of your facility. It must include issues other than the dollar loss of the items, but the dollar amount itself should include the following:

1. Temporary replacements
2. The cost of the replacements
3. Downtime
4. Discount cash
5. Insurance rate changes

It is crucial for security managers to understand the concept of criticality. When explaining any cost-benefit analysis to give reasons why you need a particular security system, make sure you explain that criticality is far more than just the direct cost of the items lost. In addition, replacement costs include the current purchase price, the costs of delivery, installation costs, any additional materials needed during the installation, and other such costs.

Using a criticality and probability spectrum allows a security manager to quantify security risks and determine which vulnerabilities merit immediate attention.

Table 1   The Probability/Criticality Matrix

Probability	*Criticality*
1. Highly Probable	A. Very Serious
2. Moderately Probable	B. Moderately Serious
3. Probable	C. Serious

Area of Hotel	*Probability*	*Criticality*	*Rank*
1. Housekeeping Storage	1	C	2B
2. Payroll Office	3	A	1C
3. Food and Beverage Storage Room	2	B	3A

Once the analysis has been completed, and the security problems have been identified and ranked in order of importance, the security manager must decide how best to proceed.

Security Survey

Regular inspections by security managers are necessary to ensure that what needs to get done is getting done. Thinking out how to prevent and minimize loss is a key principle during an internal security survey and can help a hotel document, identify, abate, and monitor problems, thereby protecting itself against loss and liability. Even though security managers generally focus on personal and property protection, both types of security survey should incorporate the following six-step internal security risk assessment process:

- Identify potential for loss or other problems.
- Analyze potential loss or significance of problems.
- Examine alternatives for viability.
- Select the best techniques.
- Implement the program.
- Monitor and improve the program.

If a hotel does not have a security manager, its management should seriously consider hiring a consultant or hotel security expert to provide such services. Surveys provide the documented proof of potential security problems and the actions that have been taken to remedy those problems. If the process identifies problems that are outside the resources of the organization, additional security help can then be justified. To ensure an objective evaluation, the person conducting the survey should have expertise in a wide range of disciplines.

In preparation for the security assessment, a review of various sources that identify vulnerabilities is helpful. The reviewers should try to get access to past security incident reports, investigative reports, police reports, statistical data, employee security surveys, industrial standards, and security literature. Some potential security risks the analysis will uncover include the following:

Simple and aggravated assault

Bomb threats and bombings

Burglary

Civil disturbance

Drug abuse

Gang activity

Gambling

Homicides

Impostors

Fraud

Kidnapping

Information loss

Robbery

Strikes

Terrorism

This security survey is intended to establish a simplified risk assessment program. It will help identify problem areas and will provide a tool for the security manager to protect the hotel from potential litigation.

Claims Management

A critical part of risk management is the development of a strong, well-organized claims management program. When developing this program, ensure that slips, trips, and falls are covered in detail and then managed very professionally. It has been proven that well-handled claims on trips, falls, and slips result in lower liability payments. One example of how this type of situation can occur is when the banquet department flashes ballroom foyer lights to "push" guests into a ballroom or function area. During the second the lights are out, a guest trips, slips, or falls, injuring himself or herself. Who is responsible—the guest who tripped or the hotel whose personnel flashed the light, causing the guest to trip? Hotels are not insurers of the public, although some people do believe this to be the case. They are, however, required to provide reasonable care to avoid the possibility of injury to others and to prevent any unreasonable risk of harm.

The time critical to a claim is the first fifteen minutes after an accident. The emergency response team is usually the group of hotel staff dealing with an injured person. Their professionalism alone may decide the fate of the hotel's liability. Proper response, documentation of the accident scene, and securing of witness evidence are crucial factors in all accidents (*Lodging*, p. 27).

When an accident does occur, the hotel management should consider comping a dinner check, for example, only as a gesture of goodwill, and ensure that it is not construed as an admission of guilt. This is mainly done in incidents involving someone who reports a food illness. Most food illness reports are assumed to be cases of salmonella. Salmonellosis is caused by single-celled bacteria common to the intestinal tract and waste of most warm-blooded animals. The symptoms include cramps, fever, vomiting, and diarrhea. The symptoms usually do not take effect until about 24 hours to two days later. Some allergic reactions, which can occur within hours of a meal, can be confused with food poisoning.

OSHA

Workplace inspections by the Occupational Safety and Health Administration (OSHA) are conducted for one of three reasons:

1. In response to a report of an accident, injury, or fatality at a hotel
2. Pursuant to a complaint by an employee alleging that a violation of the Act has occurred or is occurring
3. As part of a regular or scheduled inspection

Although there is nothing a hotel can do to avoid OSHA inspections altogether, advance preparation puts a hotel in a better position to control the direction of an inspection.

OSHA can gain access to a hotel in one of two ways: through the consent of the hotel management, in which case no search warrant is required, or through a validly executed search warrant. The security manager must keep in mind that if the scope of an OSHA inspection appears reasonable, then a judge will probably agree with its validity. Inspection warrants are rarely denied. OSHA is definitely more likely to broaden an inspection based on the fact that it had to obtain a warrant, rather than narrow its scope. If hotel managers are unsure about the legal or practical issues regarding a search warrant inspection, they should consult legal counsel.

The key issue for security managers to remember if OSHA enters with a search warrant for an inspection is that OSHA is permitted to observe areas not according to what is covered by the hotel manager's consent or by a warrant, but only what is "in plain view." Unfortunately, even what is noticed in plain view can be used to obtain a warrant authorizing OSHA to conduct a wider inspection.

Plan for the following to happen if OSHA arrives:

1. Hold an opening conference to introduce management to the inspector and have the inspector describe the details regarding the scope of the inspection.
2. Tour the hotel. A hotel employee should be with the inspector at all times: it is the hotel's right to have representation. At no time should the inspector be allowed to wander around alone. The manner and scope of an OSHA inspection will vary greatly from one hotel to another. Nevertheless, there is a common thread that runs through all OSHA inspections—the way a hotel manages an inspection will likely be critical to the scope of the inspection.

Bloodborne Pathogens

You are probably aware of the health risks posed by hypodermic syringes or condoms contaminated with the AIDS virus (HIV) or the hepatitis B virus. Until recently, many lodging facilities were unconcerned about bloodborne pathogens. That has changed as a result of the increase in incidents such as the following:

- Exposure to HIV due to improper handling of discarded soiled linens
- Punctures to housekeeping and maintenance employees from needles placed in areas such as between mattresses and box springs, under television sets or mechanical equipment

Security managers must survey at-risk scenarios with the following staff in mind:

- Health club attendants, security, or anyone likely to come in contact administering first aid, where they may encounter infected blood or other bodily fluids

- Housekeeping staff who may encounter razor blades, syringes, discarded condoms, feminine pads, soiled linens, and contaminated surfaces in a guest room
- Laundry staff who may handle soiled linens or items wrapped in bed sheets, towels, and so on

OSHA has a bloodborne pathogen standard (Code of Federal Regulations, 29 CFR 1910.1030) that covers any employee who might reasonably be expected to come into contact with human blood or other potentially infectious material.

A program of employee awareness training should include the following:

1. Give employees information on HIV and hepatitis B, transmission of viruses, and symptoms of the diseases.
2. Explain how exposure to these viruses can occur in the workplace.
3. Train employees to recognize potentially dangerous situations and treat all materials encountered in those situations as infectious.
4. Show employees safe and proper techniques for handling wastes and disinfecting surfaces.
5. Provide safety equipment such as gloves, gowns, masks, and any tool necessary to dispose of items properly.
6. Inform employees to report incidents that may constitute exposures (*Lodging*, March 1994).

OSHA Indoor Air Quality (IAQ) Standard

Specific contaminants addressed under this proposal go beyond tobacco smoke, although that is the requirement producing the most reaction. OSHA stipulates that management cannot require employees to enter an area when smoking is occurring to perform normal work duties. Other indoor contaminants covered in the proposal include automobile exhaust that may be drawn in with outdoor air being introduced to the building air exchange system. The security manager needs to evaluate the air intakes to recommend changes to systems that pose potential dangers of taking in contaminated air via vents, doors, windows, and the like. Employees of a hotel also must be informed 24 hours prior to any use of chemicals, pesticides, or other hazardous chemicals in the workplace.

Personal Protective Equipment (PPE)

Hoteliers that are not currently paying for personal protection equipment (PPE) used by their employees on the job should be aware that they could be in violation of OSHA standards and could be cited by a compliance officer. In addition, OSHA has clarified its position that employers, in the majority of cases, must provide and pay for PPE needed for a worker to do a job safely (*Compliance Magazine*, p. 5).

Americans with Disabilities Act (ADA)

Both the American Hotel and Motel Association (Educational Institute) and the National Restaurant Association have been very active in educating the lodging industry about the ADA using books, videos, seminars, and so on.

The law regarding public accommodations went into effect on January 26, 1992. Because all the provisions of the ADA will be enforced nationwide, it is vital for hoteliers to become familiar with the act. More importantly, the lodging industry must begin to formulate plans to comply with the law. The ADA is broken down into five separate parts, or "titles." Title III of the ADA "public accommodations" is the one hotels will end up dealing with most. In public accommodations, any customer expects an equal opportunity to purchase and enjoy goods or services.

According to John Salmen, the regulations implementing Title III set forth the following suggested priorities for public accommodations that cannot immediately remove all architectural and communication barriers (p. 3).

1. Provide entry access to the facility.
2. Provide access to the primary goods and services provided by the public accommodation. This includes providing accessible routes and signage. The hotel's management must determine what it believes the hotel's primary goods and services to be. For most properties, the primary goods and services are the guest rooms, meeting rooms, and restaurants. For gaming and resort properties, the casino or recreation facilities may have an equal or greater importance.
3. Provide access to public restroom facilities used by customers or guests.
4. Remove any remaining barriers to use the public accommodation's facilities.

The security manager must ensure that the above plan is prepared and carried out in full. The coordination among the chief engineer, director of rooms, and security manager must be precise to accomplish this. As a final step, the security manager also should have all projects within the hotel scrutinized with reference to the ADA to ensure compliance.

CONCLUSION

The functions associated with risk management are vast and interesting, yet require many hours of reading and familiarization with the varied programs of OSHA, ADA, claims, and so on. I would strongly recommend that security managers thoroughly educate themselves on all the above areas, as well as ensure that they have the reference material on hand in case they need data immediately. Many of these programs are technical in nature and will not be easily recitable on a day-to-day basis. Security managers also should be adaptable to these programs, never hesitating to admit when they do not have the knowledge required. That is why expert consultants in the varied fields make themselves available.

REVIEW QUESTIONS

1. List and describe the minimum steps for a risk management program.

2. Describe the purpose of a risk analysis and the importance of probability and criticality.

3. Describe the functions of OSHA and the programs associated with OSHA.

10

Fire Prevention and Emergency Planning

The Hotel and Motel Fire Safety Act is designed to produce the safest lodging properties in the world. This act went into effect on October 1, 1994, requiring that 65 percent of each federal agency's room nights be spent in properties in compliance with the law and all federally funded meetings (in whole or in part) be held in properties that meet the guidelines. The act also stipulated that by October 1, 1995, 75 percent and by October 1, 1996, 90 percent of each federal agency's room nights be spent at hotels in compliance with the law. The specific fire safety requirements of the act are that all properties desiring to continue business with the federal government must install a hard-wired, single-station smoke detector in each guest room, according to the National Fire Protection Association Standard 74. Battery-operated smoke detectors do not qualify. Properties with more than three floors must also install an automatic sprinkler system throughout the property, including all guest rooms.

This type of fire prevention matter generally is the responsibility of the security manager. The primary purpose of fire prevention equipment and emergency plans is to protect life and property within the hotel during a crisis. Most hotels have emergency plans and fire prevention equipment in place. However, more often than not, human error or failure is the root cause of life and property tragedies: Someone fails to report a hazard, or an employee disregards an emergency procedure even after he or she was trained properly.

It should be noted here that any defense against fire must be viewed in two parts. *Fire prevention*, which usually is the hotel's major preoccupation, entails the control of heat sources and the elimination or isolation of the more obviously dangerous fuels. This commendable effort to prevent fire must not, however, be undertaken at the expense of an equal effort for fire protection. *Fire protection* includes not only the equipment to control or extinguish fire, but also devices to protect the building, its contents, and particularly its occupants, in the event of fire. Fire doors, fire walls, smokeproof towers, fire safes, nonflammable rugs and furnishings, fire detector systems—all these are fire protection matters, and are essential to any fire safety program (Fischer, p. 204).

EMERGENCY PLANNING

Floods, fires, hurricanes, blizzards, tornadoes, hazardous chemical spills, and power outages are some of the disasters that pose a threat to hotels. However, because it is nearly impossible to know for certain when these disasters will strike, hotels must have an emergency plan to protect themselves from these devastating events.

Needless to say, this requires advance planning, and it can be challenging to imagine most risks. Once the risk analysis is completed, however, the security manager must determine priorities. Putting the risks in order of priority will also assist in creating a successful emergency plan. Within this plan, three separate groups of people need to be established:

1. *Operations* is made up of managerial representatives who oversee administrative issues and ensure that the emergency is being handled according to the plan.
2. *The emergency response team (ERT)*—sometimes called the HEAT, "Hotel Emergency Action Team"—actually seeks out the root cause of the emergency (i.e., fire, bomb, etc.).
3. *The logistics group* supports the rest of the hotel such as banquets personnel who assist function people in evacuating ballrooms, engineers who keep generators and other equipment operating, and others who do important parts in an emergency yet go unrecognized during the event.

It is very important that the emergency plan identify and explain the duties of each position by department for each type of emergency. The plan also should include notification sheets to make personnel aware of situations. Another vital section of the plan should be how to deal with the postemergency situation: getting affected areas cleaned up, reinstating guests into the hotel comfortably, and getting employees back to work.

The security manager should try to coordinate efforts from the "command center" to cordon off and preserve damaged areas. The task of photographing, inspecting architectural designs for defects, and adding up actual damaged property claims and estimates needs to be accomplished as quickly as possible. Only after everything has been photographed and documented should the clean-up phase begin.

Once a plan has been developed, it should be reviewed and critiqued by other management staff for accuracy. In addition, the plan should be tested at least annually. Finally, all emergency situations should be followed up with an after-action analysis describing in a positive manner the procedures followed and those done incorrectly. This analysis is a learning tool for the staff that should be used with constructive criticism.

Crisis Communication

A hotel should also have an outline within the procedures about how to handle the media. The community and others will want to know what exactly is going on. Generally, the hotel's public relations manager or spokesperson should cover at least three major points:

1. Take responsibility for the crisis and describe (if you can) what happened, when, and where within the hotel.
2. Define the impact of the crisis and the extent of the damage.
3. Describe the hotel's response to the crisis.

This information is critical to security managers because they may not be aware during the crisis that the public relations manager is talking to the media. Designated media locations are important so that interference by the press is totally eliminated. Ad hoc interviewing of employees and victims of the crisis should be prevented. The media must not be allowed to manipulate a crisis scene into a three-ring circus.

Medical Emergencies

In most states, hotels are not required to provide medical services for their guests. In busy hotels, however, a large percentage of the calls for security services will be medically related. These calls will range from simple abrasions and burns to serious trauma. Even if your hotel is in the middle of a large city with several hospitals and ambulance services, significant delays can be expected before expert assistance will arrive. Yet although many of the calls security receives in a given day will require some medical assistance, it generally will not be enough to justify the cost of a full-time physician who would need to be available twenty-four hours a day, seven days a week.

The answer is training. Security personnel, or any hotel employee who is likely to respond to calls for such services, must be properly trained. The key is to train for the level of services you are prepared to provide, and no more. Once medical assistance has commenced, you are expected to carry it out properly. The legal liabilities that arise against persons in such situations generally relate to how they performed the aid for which they were duly qualified. In short, a security officer must not attempt to perform CPR on a victim if the officer has not been certified to perform CPR. The level of training recommended for most hotels is basic first aid and CPR, both of which generally are available through the local chapter of the American Red Cross and are of nominal expense. In a very large property, some security employees can be trained as Emergency Medical Technicians (EMTs). The risk of such advanced training is that guests may come to expect it all the time, yet manpower or budget constraints may prohibit having an EMT on each shift 24 hours a day.

Evacuation Planning

Most hotels will have some level of emergency evacuation plans on hand. Whether the plans are simple or sophisticated depends on the security manager's exposure to disasters and knowledge of the subject. As mentioned earlier, the risk analysis that the security manager conducts also will include evacuation vulnerabilities. Ensuring that a hotel can handle certain crowds is easy enough; however, ensuring that you can get the crowd out safely in the event of an emergency can be challenging.

Evacuation from high-rise buildings is even more of a challenge. Usually there are only two avenues of travel up and down for high-rise buildings—elevators and stairs. The security manager must be aware that, in order to exit when an emergency occurs, human beings will naturally go toward the door through which they entered the hotel or function room. Therefore, if a hotel uses ballroom exits only in case of emergency situations, someone has to be designated to inform the patrons and guests which way to exit. These guests and patrons also do not check for a hotel's fire exits when attending events such as weddings or dances. Another contributing factor to confusion in an emergency situation is when the room or corridor the crowd is in does not have windows, as this leads to a psychological effect which disorients people as to where they are and how to exit the hotel. Hotel security departments must learn to overcome these types of problems until the time comes when elevators are made safe to use in case of an emergency (which is being reviewed at the time of writing this book).

Evacuation plans for employees need to be established and detailed information must be provided so that step-by-step plans can be offered. New employees should get a basic overview of evacuation plans during their orientation program within the first few days of employment. Additional training should be given once in a work environment or department. It is important for employees to be very comfortable within their environment, knowing the nearest exits and stairwells.

When setting up evacuation plans, review and evaluate the circumstances of the hotel and then ask a few questions:

1. Are routes to exits well lighted, fairly direct, and free of obstacles?
2. Are there signs posted on elevators to warn against their use in case of fire? Do these signs point out the direction of fire exits?
3. Are evacuation procedures provided for disabled persons?
4. Do corridors have emergency lighting in case of power failure?
5. Who makes the decision to evacuate? How will personnel be notified?
6. Who will operate the communication system? What provisions have been made in case the primary communication system breaks down? Who is assigned to provide

and receive information about the state of emergency and the progress of the evacuation? By what means? (Fischer, p. 215).

CONCLUSION

The security manager can use both monthly fire drills that train only the emergency response team and the annual evacuation drill that involves all employees, as learning tools. The more comfortable the employees and the emergency response team feel with evacuating the hotel, the greater success you will have with saving lives. Security managers must ensure that senior management budgets appropriately for these events and supports them by full participation. The reality of evacuation planning is that the more times or occasions the hotel staff and ERT perform this function, the better they will become and at the same time build up their team work.

REVIEW QUESTIONS

1. What is the Hotel and Motel Fire Safety Act?

2. Describe the types of emergencies for which a security manager should plan.

3. What role does the public relations manager have in a crisis?

11

Special Concerns and Criminal Trends

PROSTITUTION

It is probably safe to say that prostitution has been around as long as the concept of inns for travelers. Some of the comments frequently heard about prostitution is that it is a victimless crime and that society should not care what consenting adults do in privacy. However, prostitution is a problem that, if not controlled, can ruin a hotel's reputation. The word *controlled* was used intentionally, for prostitution cannot and will not ever be eliminated. The security objective should be to reduce such activity to an absolute minimum. A hotel's reputation is, without doubt, its single most important asset. No matter how professional the hotel's services may be or how good a value may be offered, no one respectable will stay at your hotel if this type of activity is allowed to take place openly.

It is not the prostitutes (both males and females) that are in and of themselves a concern, but rather the peripheral activity that frequently accompanies prostitution. Theft of the guests' property, assaults on the guests, and drugs are only a sample of the concerns associated with this crime. It is in the best interest of the hotel operator and guests alike to control prostitution.

There are a number of simple control methods a hotel can employ. First, guest registration procedures must be established and followed closely. All guests must be required to show valid photo identification such as a driver's license and preferably a credit card when checking in, even if they are paying cash in advance for their stay. The reason for the tight registration process is that most streetwalkers will not carry identification. The more sophisticated "call girl" or "escort" type of prostitute will have identification, but she or he also represents less of a threat to the innkeeper.

The second method of control can be utilized in properties that have computerized front desk procedures and can print out a complete list of all guests by room as well as list the number of occupants registered in that particular room. Once given that list, particularly at night when guests are returning to their rooms with visitors they may have just met in the local bar, the security officer can screen all incoming guests at the front door. (This works very well when hotel policy regarding visitor access after a certain hour is implemented.) This method has two benefits. First, the innkeeper is entitled as a matter of law to additional revenue if a second person is staying in the room. Second, if in fact the "visitor" is a streetwalker, not only will he or she not have identification as noted above, but the guest may not want to risk having a second person listed on the registration folio.

The final two methods of prevention include employee cooperation. The housekeeping department will know if a certain guest room has heavy traffic going to and from it and can alert security. Secondly, hotel managers must maintain a no-tolerance attitude toward prostitution while supporting security in its efforts to deal with the problem. Common meeting places for prostitutes are lobby pay telephones, bars, and easily recognized hotel fixtures such as chairs, plants, and the like.

CHECK AND CREDIT CARD FRAUD

There are two general types of problems associated with bars, restaurants, stores, and the front desk in a hotel. They are check and credit card fraud, and theft of merchandise including food and beverage items. Incidents involving "walk-outs" are common when nonpaying customers enjoy a meal and/or drinks in a hotel and then proceed to leave without offering to pay for the items consumed. Unfortunately, this type of crime is only a misdemeanor in most states and innkeepers are very limited in what they can do after the fact. Frequently, if the patron is caught leaving, they can be confronted and—if they refuse to pay—be held long enough for security or the public police to arrive. The thief then can be identified for future reference or prosecution. The amount of the loss usually is not worth the time required to prosecute, so it is recommended that the name and description of the individual be recorded and distributed to all outlets in the hotel. You may try alternate means of payment (e.g., having a family member pay, or requesting another form of payment like cash). If the person tries to obtain food or drink again, they can be refused until they pay for the previous bill.

Credit cards very often are used as a means of payment by patrons because of their convenience and the generation of tax records for business purposes. This convenience, however, has caused some problems for the hotel operator, particularly in food and beverage outlets and stores. The security department must face problems ranging from guests using stolen cards and cards over their allowable limit to dishonest employees inflating gratuities or even writing in gratuities. The best means of avoiding these and other scams is to develop detailed policies and procedures for authorization of use, and to train employees to follow the procedures. Charging store merchandise to a guest room, for example, must somehow be verified first. Management must then follow up to ensure compliance with the rules, and violators should be dealt with appropriately. If security is called to investigate alleged wrongdoing by employees and the allegations are proven, swift and severe disciplinary action should be taken after all levels of disciplinary action are considered. Disciplinary action can range from counseling to termination.

DRUGS

The sale and use of illegal drugs are major issues in any industry, but appear more complicated in the lodging industry. The innkeeper must be concerned not only with employees, but also with guests and patrons who become involved with using and selling drugs. The use of drugs by employees on or off the job presents some serious consequences for both performance and safety. With the cost of workers' compensation insurance rising so high and representing one of the largest line expenses for liability, employers must address the increased use of drugs by employees. Only recently have employers begun to consider the possibility that some employee accidents are directly related to drug use on or off the job. Even employees who do not use drugs but who are aware of others who do are affected. Morale problems are likely to arise among employees who want to do their job well, but see others not performing because of drug use. Furthermore, a work environment that allows employees to sell drugs to co-workers will create the impression that management does not care or is incompetent.

Although still controversial at this stage, employers may wish to consider the possibility of drug testing on employees who either have declining performance levels or who have exhibited unusual behavior or evidence of drug use. Legal counsel should be consulted before this action is taken. A number of legislative reforms on intoxication on the job have been enacted recently, including denying benefits (e.g., pay, holidays, contributions to 401K plans) in cases in which accidents are alcohol- or drug-related. Talk to legal counsel about your state's legislation. Effective ways to deal with substance abuse problems are complicated. The long-term solution is education and awareness, not policing employees. The hotel should have an Employee Assistance Program (EAP), which may reduce the incidents and cost of alcoholism and other abuse at work. Yet we must be realistic and acknowledge that both alcoholism and drugs do exist in the lodging industry.

Unfortunately, most hoteliers wait until drug dealing is rampant before they act on tips about drug usage. This does more harm than rapid action because, by the time management reacts to the problem, more employees are involved and affected, which may result in having to remove more staff from the hotel. Security managers also can consider using undercover investigators posing as employees to determine who the dealer and buyers are, as evidence for termination.

Drug use or sale by guests is not an unusual problem, but is one that hotel operators should be prepared to resolve. It is very unlikely that a hotel manager will be able to prevent a guest from using drugs in the privacy of his or her room. If however, the manager becomes aware of such use, action should be taken. Limited use (e.g., smoking a marijuana cigarette) may best be handled by warning the guest that repeated activity will result in removal from the hotel. However, evidence of more serious use (such as large parties with cocaine left out in the open) may require assistance from the local police. It is common for drug dealers to use large urban hotels to conduct their drug deals, for the size of the hotel usually will ensure their anonymity. Certainly, no hotel operator wants to see her or his hotel aired on the evening news as a result of a major drug bust. Liaison with local, state, and federal law enforcement agencies is vitally important. Most law enforcement arrests involving drugs occur off property; however, the legal case may be developed around the actual activity that took place while on hotel property.

Training all hotel staff about drug activity awareness will assist security in preventing illegal sales, manufacture, or use of drugs on hotel premises. All employees should be familiar with the following possible warning signs of drug activity:

- A frequent pattern of public telephone use
- A frequent pattern of people congregating in certain secluded areas in the hotel (such as specific restrooms)

- A frequent pattern of particular patrons being approached by other patrons with evidence of money, envelopes, known drug paraphernalia, or other suspicious items
- A guest who tends to tip higher than normal for services
- Guest refusal of housekeeping entrance
- Room service orders with instructions to leave the delivery in hallway
- Large amounts of cash displayed at public areas such as at front desk, near doorman, or near concierge

PROTECTION OF PUBLIC FIGURES

Depending on the size and location of a hotel, certain types of public figures are likely to stay as guests on occasion. In larger, convention-class hotels, political figures are often in attendance for social events. Public figures, whether they are politicians or people such as rock stars or sports teams, often will draw crowds. These crowds may be admirers, or they may be demonstrators protesting the appearance of the individual. In either instance, security is faced with the difficult task of controlling the crowd while protecting the public figure. One should not assume that the local police will always take care of or even be aware of these problems. Instead, the security manager should be prepared to work with the authorities in planning for the person's arrival, stay, and departure.

Planning is the key. Occasionally, hotel security will not receive any advance notice of the person's arrival. However, if your hotel security procedures include how to handle this type of scenario, coordinating this process should not take very long. Generally, though, there will be varying amounts of lead time available before the event. If this time is adequate, detailed planning will avert risk with minimal difficulty. The following are issues to address during this stage:

- *Communications systems.* Be sure all equipment is operating and rent additional radios if needed.

- *Transportation.* Plan transportation of the celebrity to and from the hotel and airport; in conjunction with their dignitary protection staff or secret service, work out alternate routes and possible escape routes from within the hotel.
- *Emergency equipment.* Have medical equipment and an ambulance, if needed, standing by.
- *Access control.* Limit bystanders' and other hotel employees' access to the areas where this person will be located. Provide for crowd control by roping off areas or using barriers.
- *Intelligence.* If this public figure recently has been at other hotels or events, contact the security and/or police in that area for any information that might be helpful in planning for the celebrity's arrival (e.g., were there demonstrators? Who were they? Was there any violence?).

Autograph Seekers and Fan Clubs

Soliciting for autographs has become an obsession for some people. Some will travel nationally just to obtain as many autographs as possible. Why? The payback on signed sports cards and memorabilia has skyrocketed and continues to rise each day. Most autograph seekers will enjoy the fun of obtaining an autograph. However, others who are die-hards will not hesitate to violate laws and a person's right to privacy simply to gain an autograph.

Therefore, the security manager must establish procedures for handling autograph seekers. First and foremost, the hotel management should determine whether to allow this activity on its property or only off its property. Second, if it is allowed in the hotel, specific locations for it must be identified. For example, you wouldn't want fans running around on guest floors. However, you might allow them to gather at the front entrance so that autographs are available when a vehicle arrives or departs. If a sports team will be staying at the hotel, be sure to ask the sales managers to have a team liaison make contact with the security manager prior to the team's arrival. The security manager can then determine if the team wants to welcome autograph seekers or not and, if not, what alternative mode of arrival they will use. A team may wish to drive straight in to a loading dock and unload only after the door has been secured. Some high-profile players may need a special escort by security. Others may not want to be disturbed while walking through a hotel lobby. Third, the security manager must determine whether trespassing or illegal solicitation laws shall be enforced and, if so, spelled out to the security staff. Look at this carefully with legal counsel, because many autograph seekers are minors and may not be subject to these laws. Caution also should be taken when deciding how to notify a parent or guardian of such activities. Finally, remember that autograph seekers can become a real nuisance if allowed to roam a hotel freely.

GUEST EVICTION

The hotel may make reasonable regulations governing the conduct of its guests, provided such regulations are applied to all persons, without discrimination. These regulations can be designed to prevent immorality, drunkenness, or any form of willful misconduct, e.g., loud obnoxious behavior, drug activity, etc., that may offend other guests, may bring the hotel into disrepute, or may be inconsistent with the generally recognized properties of life. The hotel has the right to evict any guest who willfully violates these rules. (Be sure the person is a "guest" and not a "tenant.") Obviously, the eviction must be done in a reasonable manner. If guests refuse to leave the hotel after their attention has been called to the violation and they have been requested to leave and given a reasonable opportunity to do so, the hotel may forcibly evict them. The hotel may use only such force as is reasonably necessary to accomplish this goal. Management personnel and security officers should be carefully instructed on this point and the hotel should obtain the assistance of the local police.

When a hotel guest becomes ill with a contagious disease, the hotel management, after notifying the guest that she or he must leave, has the right to remove the guest in a careful manner and at an appropriate time to a hospital or other place of safety, provided this does not imperil the guest's life. As a practical matter, however, it is preferable to consult with an attorney and report these matters to the proper local authorities. Usually the local authorities will take charge and remove the sick guest. The illness of an indigent guest should be reported to the local department of welfare, communicable diseases should be reported to the local health authorities, and psychiatric cases should be reported to the police.

COPYCAT CRIMES

Security managers must ensure that they are knowledgeable about many types of crime, with special attention to those that may occur at a hotel—even if one would normally think they are unlikely to occur. For example, a hotel shuttle bus left a hotel en route to the airport with a group of tourists and was hijacked. The hijackers, posing as guests, had boarded the bus and waited. As it pulled out of the airport, one of the men pulled a gun and ordered the driver to head in another direction while his accomplice robbed the tourists of jewelry and money at gunpoint. The more common types of copycat crime include:

- luggage stealers
- delivering a package to the hotel front desk C.O.D. for someone who has left for the day and collecting a large sum of money from the cashier for the package, which when opened contains something of little value such as a brick

- a criminal entering the hotel, claiming to be the spouse of so-and-so and asking for a room key

SEXUAL HARASSMENT

Just because managers do not hear about sexual harassment does not mean that there isn't a problem. All too often, people who suffer from sexual harassment feel that it must be their own fault. Because they blame themselves, they do not report the situation to management. The lodging industry must take steps to ensure that all employees are aware of their rights and of the need to report all incidents. Management also needs to remember that legally the hotel is responsible (liable) for the acts of its employees. (This responsibility is called "respondeat superior.") Therefore, make sure there is a hotel policy on this subject, procedures for investigation methods, and documentation to defend all actions. The security manager also should remember that victim sensitivity training for all employees will play a key role in resolving this type of incident. If the hotel has a policy handbook, it is essential to put the procedure in writing so that all employees are aware that this type of behavior is unacceptable in the workplace.

CONCLUSION

The lodging industry is changing daily and must keep pace with corporate America if it is to continue to grow. It is essential to ensure that hotel staff at all levels stay knowledgeable about all the issues mentioned in this chapter, as well as keeping up with technology. The industry must work hard to maintain the talent we have and not lose those persons to other industries. Education and training once again prove to be a vital link in this effort. The importance of well-educated and very diverse staff cannot be overemphasized.

REVIEW QUESTIONS

1. How can we prevent "the oldest profession in the world" from continuing to occur in hotels?

2. Describe the type of policy and procedure a hotel should implement to prevent credit card and check fraud.

3. What must be done in order for a hotel to have a drug-free workplace?

12

Legal Issues

INTRODUCTION

There are so many different circumstances in which a hotel may be liable that entire texts have been dedicated to discussing these vulnerabilities. This situation is due to the general nature of the lodging industry business and the myriad of services it offers. In effect, hotel operators (innkeepers) are telling prospective customers to stay with them overnight, bring their family and their car, eat, drink, and use all the hotel's facilities while they are guests. Essentially, the guests are encouraged to entrust their valuables and personal safety to the hotel. The hotel operator has implicitly or explicitly assured the guests that they will have a safe overnight stay, and that the hotel shall be the guests' humble abode for the duration of their stay.

This chapter will explore only the most common types of liability problems. In the traditional role of hotel security, concerns for or involvement with a liability problem usually was a result of coincidence. Management often was reluctant to involve security because it had questionable confidence in the staff. Instead, it handled liability issues in a public relations fashion. With the phenomenal growth of litigation throughout society, and particularly in the lodging industry, security has taken on major responsibility to investigate, report, and develop prevention programs for many of these problems. Hence, it makes considerable sense, for example, for the contemporary hotel security manager to be responsible for overseeing and managing most general liability problems, including the loss of guest property, claims of guest injury, damage to or loss of guest vehicles, and employee accidents. (Although handling workers' compensation should be the responsibility of the human resources department, all injury reports need to be handled as investigations shared with security.) The security department should be the first department to which losses and injuries are reported. If so, chances are better that information gathered by a security officer during the initial stages will be the most reliable, and that the methods of data collection will be controlled with the greatest consistency.

GUEST PROPERTY

The most common claim guests make against a hotel is that some of their property has been stolen from their guest room. Security personnel must be cautioned not to assume that all reports of lost property necessarily mean that the property has been stolen. It may simply be misplaced or missing. It is common for victims of loss to blame someone else. Therefore, adequate information must be gathered to determine whether the item was in fact stolen or simply misplaced by the guest. The reason is obvious—lost property requires one type of investigative approach, while stolen property involves another.

To determine whether a claim of stolen guest property is valid, a number of steps must be taken while filling out an incident report:

1. Gather all pertinent information (who, what, where, when, why, and how) on the incident.

2. Search room or scene for property; sometimes a fresh pair of eyes searching helps (search guest room, hallways, trash cans, closets, elevator foyers, plants, and so on).
3. Inspect all door frames and doors, locking mechanisms, floors, windows, walls, and ceilings for signs of forced entry. Be sure to photograph all signs of entry and collect any loose material, e.g., wood chips, metal shavings, in evidence bags, ensuring that a measurement tool (ruler) is used in all photos, depicting size of markings.
4. Interrogate door lock if hotel has an electronic key system.
5. Obtain a copy of guest folio (printout of guest activity while in hotel) and registration card.
6. Gather copies of all department schedules to discover who may have had access to area or room (i.e., housekeeping, room service, engineering, guest services, etc.).
7. Interview and interrogate all employees who had access to guest room.
8. Inspect all employee lockers and baggage for guest property.
9. File police report.

These prerequisites must be met before the security investigator can present all the facts to the security manager. Once all this information is gathered, the security manager can determine what action the hotel will take (i.e., to pay damages or deny liability for the loss; see sample letters, figures 12-1 and 12-2).

Guest status must be established by verifying that the individual was in fact a guest of the hotel at the time the loss occurred. Such status is important: case law has been clear that, without the requisite status, the standard of care due to the individual is not as great, and therefore liability will be less likely. The reasoning behind this guest status was given in the 1957 case of *Idelman-Danziger, Inc. v. Statler Mgmt.*, 136 A2nd 119. The court noted that "to establish the relationship of innkeeper and guest, the parties must intend to do so; the person

July 12, 1995

Mark Beaudry
777 West 2nd Street
New York, NY 10011

Dear Mr. Beaudry,

I was very concerned to learn about your reported
missing brown tri-fold wallet on June 10, 1995. Our
investigation to date has not recovered your missing
property, however, in the event that we are able to recover
it I will notify you.

I would like to suggest that you contact your homeowner
insurance carrier for coverage. The Best Hotel cannot accept
responsibility for personal or company property not checked
with us or otherwise not placed in our care, custody and
control. The hotel does provide our guests with safes for
storage of all valuables at no charge.

I sincerely regret that this incident marred your stay in
Chicago and caused you any inconvenience.

Sincerely,

John Smith
Director of Safety & Security

File# 011-95

Figure 12-1. Sample Missing Property Response Letter

July 14, 1995

Mark Beaudry
777 West 2nd Street
New York, NY 10011

Dear Mr. Beaudry,

I was very concerned to learn of your reported damaged vehicle.

I have concluded my investigation into this matter and after interviewing hotel valets as well as viewing our hotel camera system, I have not found any wrongdoing by the hotel.

In addition, The Best Hotel cannot accept responsibility for reported damage to a vehicle after the vehicle has left the premises. As our claim ticket does indicate, all claims must be submitted prior to departure.

I sincerely regret that this incident marred your stay with us and caused you any inconvenience.

Please call me should you have any questions.

Sincerely,

John Smith

John Smith
Director of Safety & Security

File# 011-95

Figure 12-2. Sample Damaged Vehicle Response Letter

accommodated must be received as guest and must procure accommodations in that capacity, although it is not essential that he/she register."

Reports of property left at a hotel after checkout should be logged chronologically for reference, in case the guest's property is recovered (this log can be titled "Nonliability Log"). It is important for all departments to refer these calls to security. Most guests have a tendency to contact either the housekeeping department or the front desk.

Another concern is whether the guest's allegedly stolen property was in the custody of the innkeeper at the time it disappeared. The legal doctrine *infra hospitium*, meaning "within the inn," indicates that the property of a guest must either come within the walls of the inn or come under the innkeeper's care. It is thus a rule of *care and custody* (*Davidson* v. *Madison Corp.*, 247 NYS 789, 795 (1931)). Care and custody more commonly arise under the concept of *bailment*, which is defined by *Black's Law Dictionary*, Revised Fifth Edition, as follows:

> A delivery of goods or personal property, by one person to another, in trust for the execution of a special object upon or in relation to such goods, beneficial either to the bailor or bailee or both, and upon a contract, express or implied, to perform the trust and carry out such object, and thereupon to redeliver the goods to the bailor or otherwise dispose of the same in conformity with the purpose of the trust. (p. 461)

Basically, the nature of a bailment is the entrustment of one person's property to another. Traditionally, the courts have held innkeepers absolutely liable for any losses sustained by guests while at a hotel with the intent of protecting the guest/traveler from the dishonesty or negligence of the innkeeper or the hotel employees. In response to what amounts to strict liability for guest property, innkeepers have been aided by most states' legislatures, which have enacted legislation limiting liability for guest property to a fixed amount. This amount varies from state to state (e.g., $300 in Massachusetts; see example card, figure 12-3).

Notice to Guests

State Laws

Chapter 140, Section 10 to 13 Inclusive, Laws of Massachusetts

Section 10. "An innholder shall not be liable for losses sustained by a guest except of wearing apparel, articles worn or carried on the person, personal baggage and money necessary for traveling expenses and personal use, nor shall such guest recover of an innholder more than three hundred dollars as damages for any such loss; but an innholder shall be liable in damages to an amount not exceeding one thousand dollars for the loss of money, jewels and ornaments of a guest specially deposited for safe keeping, or offered to be so deposited, with such innholder, person in charge at the office of the inn, or other agent of such innholder authorized to receive such deposit. This section shall not affect the innholder's liability under any special contract for other property deposited with him for safe keeping after being fully informed of its nature and value, nor increase his liability in case of loss by fire or overwhelming force beyond that specified in the following section."

Section 11. "In case of loss by fire or overwhelming force, innholders shall be answerable to their guest only for ordinary and reasonable care in the custody of their baggage and other property."

Section 12. "Whoever puts up at a hotel, motel, inn, lodging house or boarding house and, without having an express agreement for credit, procures food, entertainment or accommodation without paying therefor, and with intent to cheat or defraud the owner or keeper thereof; or, with such intent, obtains credit to a hotel, motel, inn, lodging house or boarding house for such food, entertainment or accommodation by means of any false show of baggage or effects brought thereto; or with such intent, removes or causes to be removed any baggage or effects from a hotel, motel, or inn while in lien exists thereon for the proper charges due from him for fare and board furnished therein, shall, if the value of food, entertainment or accommodation exceeds one hundred dollars, be punished by imprisonment in a jail or house of correction for not more than two years, or by a fine of not more than six hundred dollars, or if the value of the food, entertainment or accommodation does not exceed one hundred dollars, shall be punished by imprisonment for not more than one year or by a fine of not more than one thousand dollars; and whoever, without having an express agreement for credit, procures food or beverage from a common victualler without paying therefor and with intent to cheat or defraud shall be punished by a fine of not more than five hundred dollars. or by imprisonment for not more than three months."

Proof that such food, entertainment, accommodations or beverage, or credit for the same, was obtained by a false show of baggage or effects, or that such baggage or effects were removed from any such place by any person while such lien existed thereof without an express agreement permitting such removal, or if there was not an express agreement for credit, that payment for such food, entertainment, accommodation or beverage was refused upon demand, shall be presumptive evidence of the intent to cheat or defraud referred to herein."

Section 13: "Innholders shall post a printed copy of this and the three preceding sections in a conspicuous place in each room of their inns."

MASSACHUSETTS HOTEL-MOTEL ASSOCIATION

Figure 12-3.   Sample (Typical) State Innkeeper Law

Determination of fault also varies: some states require that the claimant prove negligence on the innkeeper's part, while other states simply require that claimants prove they were guests (see guest statutes above) at the time of the loss and that an item or items were indeed missing. An innkeeper and his or her security manager should be familiar with the governing statutes of the state. In addition to amounts and issues of fault, most states require hotels who want the benefit of the limited liability to post a copy of the statute for each guest to view and therefore be "put on notice" or made aware of such limitations. For the most part, these statutes traditionally have been posted within a guest room (e.g., on the back of a door or on the closet wall).

The legislatures have passed such laws because of how difficult it is for innkeepers to prevent crimes involving personal property, and because of the likelihood of fraudulent claims (*Morris* v. *Hotel Riviera, Inc.*, 704 F.2nd 1113 (1983)). Although the validity of these statutes has been challenged on numerous occasions, including in the Morris case cited above, the courts have consistently upheld the statutory limits, even when the claims were for losses of thousands of dollars.

A few precautions for the security manager follow:

1. Be sure that the statute was in fact posted at the time of the loss.
2. Determine if the claimant had guest status.
3. Establish whether the allegedly stolen property was "within the hotel" to determine the innkeeper's degree of care, custody, and control.

GUEST INJURIES

Guest injuries are common occurrences and result from a variety of hazards including, but not limited to, the following:

Wet floors

Worn carpets

Exposed carpet tacks

Broken furniture

Electrical wires improperly laid along a floor

Broken glass not vacuumed up

Poor lighting

Lack of directions for equipment usage

Inadequate Security

The type of guest injury claim of greatest concern to security professionals is allegation of unsafe conditions based on the argument that the hotel had inadequate security protection. Following the publicity received by the so-called "Connie Francis" case, *Garzilli* v. *Howard Johnson's Motor Lodges., Inc.*, 419 F. Supp. 1210 (1976), there has been a continuous string of similar cases against hotels for injuries guests received as a result of attacks by third-party criminals. It is fair to say that this is a popular theory of liability now that the public is aware of the necessity for security protection in a hotel and lacks tolerance for levels of protection perceived as inadequate.

An innkeeper has the duty to exercise reasonable care for guests. If a hotel is experiencing an increase in crime, or if the surrounding neighborhood is having problems with crime in a way that could affect the hotel's guests, the innkeeper must respond to that threat by improving or increasing security measures. If the innkeeper fails to do so, he or she may be liable for any injuries guests suffer at the hands of third-party criminals. (Note: These injuries can be in the form of both physical harm and mental anguish.) Even if the offender is not caught, but the injury occurred in or immediately adjacent to the hotel's property, the hotel may be required to pay for damages.

Liability in these cases is predicated on the theory of negligence, in that it was reasonably foreseeable that the injury would occur if corrective action were not taken. If the innkeeper knew or should have known of the threat, the "reasonable care" rule will apply, establishing that the innkeeper had a duty to protect the guests, failed to do so, and as a result the guest was harmed. Remember, the objective of security should be "the protection of life and property." Therefore, the focus should be on preventing a loss in the first place. In view of this, the innkeeper, through her or his security department, must keep informed of recent trends or changes in crime patterns both within the hotel and in the surrounding neighborhood. A positive working relationship with the local police is essential for a regular flow of information regarding crime in the neighborhood. The security department's reporting system should include both monthly and semiannual reports that summarize all criminal activity for the time period covered and make everyone aware of emerging patterns of changes. Many ILSSA chapters are developing city-wide networking systems so that hotels can communicate about crime incidents in their area.

What is adequate security? There is no acceptable answer to that question, due to the lack of any established industry standards. (Note: Through the American Society of Testing and Materials (ASTM), a committee has been formed to draft specific security standards for the lodging industry.) Presently, because there are no standards, the courts are making the determination of "adequacy" on a case-by-case basis. One rule of thumb is to look at other hotels that are similarly situated geographically and are of similar size to try to assess what is acceptable within a given community. This comparison is referred to as the "community standard" and is also used by the courts to evaluate the hotel being sued. However, community standards can be misleading if it can be shown that the entire industry was below acceptable levels of protection, considering the magnitude of crime problems and the comparative cost of preventive measures. Lawsuits that claim inadequate security by property owners and managers feature a number of factors that result in a finding for the plaintiff. These include

- A history of neighborhood crime
- Inadequate security of exterior areas, parking facilities, and common interior areas
- Lack of training of front desk employees

- Poor access control and lock and key control
- Inadequate guest room security
- Negligent hiring practices
- Improper training and supervision of security personnel
- Negligent management policies

ALCOHOL SERVER LIABILITY

Alcohol server liability is a form of third-party liability. It arises when the server of alcoholic beverages is held liable for the actions of intoxicated persons who consumed alcoholic beverages in the liquor serving establishment, and as a result of the intoxication caused injury to themselves or another person. Alcohol liability problems generally do not involve security staff initially, for it is usually food and beverage department employees such as bartenders, waitresses, and managers who are directly in control of and responsible for alcohol consumption. Security does have a function to perform, however, in helping to prevent intoxicated patrons from driving a vehicle or becoming injured while walking around the hotel property. Not all alcohol liability cases are limited to motor vehicle accidents. Guests can become injured by falling down due to intoxication in an otherwise safe area. Unfortunately, in such cases the innkeeper is not able to claim the defense that it was the guest's intoxication that caused the injury, if it was the innkeeper who allowed the individual to get drunk in the first place.

The greatest risk of alcohol liability arises when the guest attempts to leave the hotel and drive a car. If a security officer is called for assistance in such circumstances, everything possible should be done to discourage the guest from driving. A hotel's management may even want to consider the extreme measures of refusing to return the guest's keys or calling the local police department. This action may cause other problems (such as difficulties regarding the inappropriateness of refusing to give a person back his or her property), but the hotel operator must weigh the risks and decide on the safest option.

Security frequently receives calls from bartenders who need assistance discontinuing service to a guest who, in the bartender's opinion, has had enough to drink. The security officer must respond promptly to such calls, for the situation is apt to get out of hand quickly. Once the security officer has arrived, she or he should obtain all relevant information from the bartender and, without question, back up the decision to discontinue service. Security should never try to overrule the server's decision. The same rule applies to any member of management who is called in for assistance in such circumstances.

For the subsequent report and follow-up investigation, it is essential to obtain all pertinent facts, names and addresses of witnesses, and documentation (e.g., bar tabs and statements) for future reference. All this information should be maintained in a file for at least the time of your state's statute of limitation.

Finally, it must always be remembered that reports, logs, and other documents are subject to legal review. The accuracy of each incident's facts is crucial to the hotel and its reputation.

HOLD HARMLESS AGREEMENTS

The security manager should consult with legal counsel and develop standard hold harmless agreements to be used by catering and convention service personnel. If the sales department is doing a thorough job, it will be able to conduct a group history, and hence be aware of any potential concerns during the actual booking of a convention. The security manager must be made aware of any potential groups that might have additional security needs. This has proven necessary in light of the Tailhook case against the Las Vegas Hilton.

The Tailhook Association is a group of navy pilots. (The term "Tailhook" comes from the hook on the back of aircraft that land on aircraft carriers. When such planes land, this hook catches on a cord stretched across the deck, and the aircraft is jerked to a halt.) The Tailhook Association had held an annual convention at the Las Vegas Hilton for 19 years. After the 1991 convention, a scandal erupted. The gist of it was that male navy pilots had sexually assaulted female pilots and that an attempted cover-up by navy officials followed.

One victim, Ms. Coughlin, filed suit, which finally reached trial in September 1994. Her claim was that the Hilton could have reasonably foreseen that male navy pilots would molest their female counterparts and failed to take steps to prevent them from doing so. From a legal standpoint, the issue boiled down to the single issue of hotels owing their guests a duty of reasonable care. *Reasonable care* is determined by weighing several factors: the possibility of injury, the gravity of any injury that might occur, the cost of protecting against the injury, and the social utility of such precautions.

The undisputed testimony in the trial established the following facts. The Tailhook Association Convention consisted of symposiums and exhibits during the day and, on Sunday night, September 7, 1991, a dinner followed by a party on the hotel's third floor. The rooms there were used as hospitality suites. Each room had access to the outside, so crowding on the floor did not present an evacuation problem. At its height, there were approximately 5,000 people at the party. The third floor covered about three acres, meaning that each person had 26 square feet of space, on average, at the peak of the party. In other words, the party was crowded, but it was not a packed, dance-floor atmosphere where no one could move. People were milling around in the hallway, walking in and out of the suites, drinking, and having a good time.

In the 18 years preceding the 1991 Tailhook Convention, there had been only one report even remotely suggesting sexual molestation. In 1988, a report was made to the Hilton security staff by a female guest that her blouse had been ripped. She did not request that the Hilton follow up the incident, and she did not report it to Las Vegas police. Previous Tailhook parties were, however, known by the Hilton to become rowdy, and there was a history of property damage. The Tailhook Association had always reimbursed Hilton for any damage.

The 1991 party was similar to others in that there was rowdiness, loudness, damage, and drunkenness. However, contrary to some press reports, the Hilton did not violate its own policy against serving liquor to inebriated guests. The Tailhook Association supplied its own liquor and the Hilton did not serve it.

At the time of the 1991 convention, the Hilton had approximately 100 security officers on its force. (The only larger security force in Las Vegas was the police department.) On the night in question, there were 30 officers on duty. These officers were connected to each other by lapel microphones. Further, the security office was able to contact the police within seconds. Hilton maintained standard operating procedures of logging all complaints on a blotter (similar to a police blotter) to keep a contemporaneous record, requiring its officers to log any out-of-the-ordinary incident, and requiring its security officers to make follow-up reports in detail and in writing. These reports were, in turn, logged by sequential numbers to assure that no report was lost from the system.

The normal security provided by the Hilton consisted of one officer patrolling a maximum of 10 floors. In consultation with the Tailhook Association, the Hilton assigned three uniformed security officers to patrol the third floor during the party. Each of these officers communicated to navy officers known as "blue shirts" who served as liaisons during the party. The Hilton did not delegate its duty to provide reasonable security to the "blue shirts" but, as in most cases, needed contact persons within the association during the event. Yet Coughlin testified that she never reported the incident to the Hilton security department. The Hilton did not challenge her account of this incident. The Hilton's position was that because Coughlin, a naval officer herself, could not have foreseen—and, by her own testimony, did not foresee—the attack despite her intelligence, training, and knowledge of the service of which she was a member, the Hilton could not reasonably have been expected to foresee that attack either, especially since there was no evidence of such conduct in prior years (*Lodging*, April 1995).

The Hilton Hotels Corp. was ordered to pay Ms. Coughlin $5 million in punitive damages and $1.7 million in compensatory damages for neglecting to protect her from sexual attacks.

REVIEW QUESTIONS

1. Describe the difference between a liability and nonliability for a hotel under the care and custody rule.

2. Why is it so important to post state innkeeper laws?

3. What is the difference between adequate and inadequate security?

13

Casino Security

In the early 1990s, the legal and social acceptance of gambling and commercial gaming increased substantially in the United States, Canada, most of Europe, Australia, and New Zealand, as well as in various developing countries. In turn, the gaming industries have become increasingly sophisticated and legitimate to reflect this reality.

The type of emerging commercial gaming activity that has the greatest relevance to the lodging industry is casino gaming, especially destination resort casino gaming. Casinos have been historically identified with exotic venues such as Las Vegas, Monte Carlo, and others. However, casino legalization and authorization increasingly has become part of a broader revenue and marketing strategy for many types of organizations, including hotel companies.

It is important to realize that there are various types of casinos that have emerged with the proliferation of legal gaming. Casinos are being developed in historic or refurbished structures, and river boats are being used to operate as floating casinos or moored casinos. There are also casinos in purpose-built facilities, which may have limited nongaming amenities. Casinos seem to be appearing most near leisure and tourist settings.

The question most often asked about gambling and hotels is whether the public policies regarding "morally suspect" activities can be expected to increase. On the one hand, with gambling, there has been a trend toward allowing people to have greater control over their choice of activities and to be more responsible for the consequences of their own actions. But this principle has not been applied uniformly over the so-called "vices" such as alcohol, tobacco, illicit drug use, prostitution, and pornography. These vices have economic and social impacts on the hotel and/or casino similar to the impacts of gambling. The likelihood of these vices being introduced into the casino is very high.

Security managers should study their local gambling and lottery ordinances to find out what is and is not allowed. In addition, they should check with their local public prosecutor to find out what cases he or she is willing to act on and how the courts interpret gambling statutes. It is a known fact that the gamblers as well as persons who attempt to conduct scams are all well-versed in gambling laws. Don't be surprised to find people who attempt to challenge casino games, testing the parameters in order to commit acts which may be on the legal borderline. Likewise, don't be afraid to ask for help from a gaming investigator in identifying marginal cases.

Emerging casino security practices, using CCTV equipment, call for gaming machines and tables to be individually identified with a location mark and casino logo. The identification, coupled with video recordings, allows taped incidents to be admitted as evidence in gaming commission hearings as well as in court. The casino security strategy is people-watching, which is nothing new. Employee theft is not new, either, especially when millions of dollars pass through the hands of employees each day. As visitors and employees come up with new ways to cheat, many eyes should be watching.

The most effective deterrent is people watching people, with most watchers out of sight. Hundreds of cameras can be hidden inside domes or behind ceiling panels. Pan/tilt capabilities, color monitors, and strategic placement all contribute to cover every square foot of a casino floor. It is important for security staff to study what they see on those cameras to determine if angles should be changed, people should be followed, or if a zoom shot should be taken of a pile of chips. Most states allow tapes from casino crimes to be admissible as court evidence. However, to ensure the tapes' validity, be sure that the machines and tables are marked with assigned numbers and logos as mentioned above (*Security*, July 1994).

RIVER BOATS

Today's river boats differ significantly from those of earlier times. Although many feature entertainment and food and beverage service, the focus is predominantly on gambling. When river boats feature casinos, the cruise experience is often sacrificed. In addition, crowding is a problem, due to the fact that river boat designers cram as many gaming positions onto each boat as possible, to take advantage of the enormous revenues generated from each position. One advantage to river boat owners is the fact that the boat is cruising—therefore, passengers do not have the option of leaving and frequently gamble more than they normally would.

To alleviate the risks associated with congested spaces, security needs to be involved in the floor planning stage of construction to ensure that foot traffic patterns and passenger movement have been considered. Another concern is that air circulation is poor in crowded spaces, and smoke-filled air can become an irritant, leading to a less-than-optimal gaming experience for many guests. Some states, such as Mississippi, offer "dockside gaming." The state maintains that the casinos must float; however, they can be permanently moored and are not required to make excursions (*Lodging*, April 1994, pp. 94–100).

Surveillance is very important in casino security environments, where criminals range from casino dealers and employees to "railbirds" who steal chips from the sides of tables while patrons are not paying attention. Surveillance specialists look for targets of theft where the stakes are high. Crimes take place in areas of intense action, where more chips are being played or the value of the game is high. Surveillance specialists also look out for known troublemakers and have a central supervisor or pit boss for every ten tables.

CURRENT ISSUES AND CONCERNS

Most casino security operations I have had the benefit of observing have highly talented staff members who can observe many tables simultaneously and are capable of identifying criminal acts being committed. Usually, the staff working in surveillance security have worked in hotel security and are knowledgeable enough about guests' traits and mannerisms to assist them in identifying problem people.

Another issue for casino security is that the budget needs are far greater than most security departments', due to the vast amount of technology necessary to conduct professional surveillance operations. Storage of video equipment, for example, is an important factor because tapes must be retained in case they are needed for prosecution of criminals or other legal matters. Par stock of replacement equipment also is critical to ensure immediate replacement of any piece of the technology that breaks down.

Most surveillance specialists are concerned about having updated and timely identification of known criminals, along with their method of operation. Knowing about these techniques is crucial to casino security professionals and will keep them keen on typical tricks of the trade. One way in which the surveillance specialist can be made aware of these criminals and their methods is through networking systems set up in cities with casinos to share information about incidents that occur at various sites. This networking system can communicate by fax, telephone, or other methods.

The relationship and coordination between the specialist operating the surveillance equipment and the security officer on the casino floor is also crucial. When a criminal act occurs, the surveillance specialist may only have a split second to notify the security officer so that he or she can take position to prevent the criminal from leaving the premises. Some casino security officers are armed and have county sheriff police powers. If so, a casino may be able to make its own arrests.

CONCLUSION

The casino industry is growing larger as each day passes and is being associated with hotels. Security managers fortunate enough to work with either the hotel side or the casino side at hotel chains need to ensure that they are familiar with gaming regulations and related laws. As mentioned earlier, some of the larger hotels that have a Vice President of Security position will usually have a security manager for the hotel and a surveillance manager for the casino. Casino security and hotel security, as professions, need to be recognized as excellent career paths that offer upward movement. These positions develop special talents that should be rewarded accordingly. Both education and experience must be continuous and security professionals must be allowed to grow with the industry. Hotel chains that have surveillance experts need to allow them to assist the industry as it grows by sharing information, training, knowledge, because it is not a competitive area. All lodging security professionals have the same goal in mind: to prevent crime from occurring in their casinos and hotels.

REVIEW QUESTIONS

1.   How is CCTV equipment utilized in the casino industry?

2. Describe the trend through which casinos are being estab-
    lished.

3. Casino surveillance has typically been a closed profession.
    Why is it important for casino security experts to share their
    knowledge with professional hotel security managers?

14

Beyond the Year 2000

In the past five years, proprietary security has grown in the lodging industry even though some hotel chains have gone through down-sizing. Most hotels cannot afford to reduce their security staff nor risk the legal ramifications that would result from a negative incident. As stated earlier, hotel owners are very intelligent people who realize that the protection of life and property is costly but necessary. Any hotel, regardless of its size, has security measures; at the very least, the staff are security-minded.

Furthermore, many guests today have become frequent and savvy travelers and know about personal safety measures. Many hotels now complement this knowledge with travel tip cards and in-room video programs containing security reminders.

ADVANTAGES OF LODGING SECURITY DEPARTMENTS

Today's lodging security professionals are having a tremendous impact on the reduction of crime in many cities, as well as helping the legal system identify the types of criminal activity within the travel and tourism industry. Given this fact, it is essential that both the public law enforcement agencies and the criminal justice system realize the importance of private security in the lodging industry.

The continuous efforts of visionaries in lodging security have had a great impact on how hotel security is perceived by others. If this positive outlook continues, the profession will develop and be recognized as a vital contributor to the security vocation as a whole. Since the profession has united through organizations such as the International Lodging Safety and Security Association, American Society for Industrial Security, and the American Hotel and Motel Security Committee, the interest has intensified. Security professionals are proud to assist in any way they can as lodging security grows.

The professionalization and success of the industry are affected by two main factors: state-of-the-art technology and traditional security presence through patrolling and guest contact. Security managers must never forget, however, that if criminals want to spend the time to defeat a security barrier, they will probably be successful. What we must try to do is to reduce the imaginable ways in which technology and human patrols can be manipulated or overcome. A security manager can virtually eliminate any target's probability of being defeated. However, crime will continue because all vulnerabilities take time to identify and eliminate.

Today's lodging security managers are continually compiling procedures to prevent future incidents from occurring. Sometimes through others' mishaps, they can learn not to have the same type of situation occur in their hotel, or at least prepare for it in case it does occur.

Finally, the future role of our technology is so vast that even we can't imagine its potential. Our efforts will be supplemented through methods of access control, surveillance, communication technology, and computers. The most important goal is the positive assurance of a safe and secure environment for our guests and patrons. If we make steps toward this goal, criminals will have to go elsewhere to find softer targets of opportunity, and the lodging industry will not be haunted by the negative impact of crimes on persons or hotel property.

The future of lodging security is very positive. Professionalization of our field is being pursued by many visionaries, and the owners of hotels realize the growing importance of security. Security managers must take the time to develop strategic plans that will bring their hotel into the year 2000 and beyond. The lodging security occupation is a promising one for the talented person who wishes to bring the profession forward through education, training, and a vision.

Appendix A

FIRE ALARM REPORT

Incident #_____

DAY:_____ DATE:_____ TIME:_____

LOCATION:_____

DEVICE:_____

Alarm sounded on floor of incident, floor above and below: Yes_____ No_____

General Alarm Sounded: Yes_____ No_____ Time:_____

Time of Fire Department Arrival:_____ Chief:_____

Time of "All Clear" by Fire Department:_____

Time Emergency Response Team Notified:_____

Manager:_____

Security Supervisor:_____

Security Officer:_____

Security Officer:_____

Engineer:_____

Engineer:_____

Time Management Notified:_____

Managing Director:_____

Operations Manager:_____

Building Superintendent:_____

Director of Security:_____

NARRATIVE:_____

_____

_____

_____

FIRE ALARM CRITIQUE

1. DATE:_____

2. TIME:_____

3. LOCATION OF MEETING:_____

4. CONDUCTED BY:_____

5. ATTENDED BY:_____

_____

_____

6. ABSENT:_____

7. COMMENT ON INCORRECT RESPONSE OR MECHANICAL FAILURE:_____

_____

_____

8. CORRECTIVE MEASURES TAKEN:_____

_____

_____

9. COMMENTS:_____

_____

_____

S/S_____   **A/M**_____

Distribution of Report within 24 Hours to:

    Original: Director of Safety and Security
        Copy: Executive Office

Revised 9/94

Appendix B

CONTRACTOR SIGN IN/OUT

DATE:_____

T/I	NAME	COMPANY	BADGE #	T/O

7/94

EXIT SIGN CHECKLIST

FLOOR	LOCATION	OK	BULB	GLASS	CASING
36	Opposite Stairway #1				
	Opposite Stairway #2				
	Next to Room #3619				
	Next to Room #3613				
35	Opposite Stairway #1				
	Opposite Stairway #2				
	Next to Room #3519				
	Next to Room #3513				
34	Opposite Stairway #1				
	Opposite Stairway #2				
	Next to Room #3419				
	Next to Room #3413				
33	Opposite Stairway #1				
	Opposite Stairway #2				
	Next to Room #3319				
	Next to Room #3313				
32	Opposite Stairway #1				
	Opposite Stairway #2				
	Next to Room #3219				
	Next to Room #3213				
31	Opposite Stairway #1				
	Opposite Stairway #2				
	Next to Room #3119				
	Next to Room #3113				

4/93

DAY:_____ DATE:_____ TIME:_____

S/O_____ S/S_____

EXIT SIGN CHECKLIST

FLOOR	LOCATION	OK	BULB	GLASS	CASING
2	Store Staircase				
Lobby	Lobby Staircase				
	At Stairway #4				
	Door to Stairway #4				
1	Over Greeter Stand				
Main	Revolving Doors				
	Revolving Doors				
	Main Entrance				
	Kitchen Entrance				
	Upper Bar				
	Lower Bar				
	Rear Door				
	Telephone Bank				
	Rotunda Exit				
	Over Greeter Stand				
	Employee Entrance				
M.E.	Over Glass Doors				
	Over Glass Doors				
	Next to Planters				
	Rotunda Side Door				
	Rotunda Side Door				
Garage	At Stairway #7				
Upper	At Stairway #2				
Level	At Stairway #1				

4/93

S/S_____

EXIT SIGN CHECKLIST

FLOOR	LOCATION	OK	BULB	GLASS	CASING
Garage	At Steam Room Door				
Lower	At Stairway #2				
Level	At Switchgear Room				
	Outside Pump Room				
	At Stairway #7				
Motor	Inside Stairway #2				
Ent.	Inside Stairway #1				
	Totals:				
	Floors 8-38 116				
	Floor 7 22				
	Floor 6 0				
	Floor 5 10				
	Floor 4 26				
	Floor 3 34				
	Floor 2 13				
	Floor 1 17				
	Garage & M.E. 10				
	Grand Total 248				

4/93

S/S_____

Appendix D

Incident#_____

FUNCTION ROOM FIRE/LIFE SAFETY CHECKLIST

FUNCTION ROOM/AREA:_____

DAY:_____ DATE:_____ TIME:_____

1. <u>FIRE EXITS, STAIRWELLS, SERVICE CORRIDORS</u>:   CLEAR_____   OBSTRUCTED_____

PERSON NOTIFIED:_____ DEPARTMENT:_____

TIME:_____ OBSTRUCTION CORRECTED:_____ TIME:_____

2. <u>FIRE EXTINGUISHERS, STANDPIPES, SPRINKLER HEADS</u>: CLEAR_____OBSTRUCTED_____

PERSON NOTIFIED:_____ DEPARTMENT:_____

TIME:_____ OBSTRUCTION CORRECTED:_____ TIME:_____

3. <u>GENERAL SAFETY HAZARDS</u>:   _____

_____

PERSON NOTIFIED:_____ DEPARTMENT:_____

TIME:_____ OBSTRUCTION CORRECTED:_____ TIME:_____

4. <u>MOBILE COOKING STATIONS (STERNO, GAS, ELECTRIC, OTHER)</u>:   NUMBER:_____

FIRE EXTINGUISHER PRESENT:_____ POSITIONED BY:_____

_____   _____
       SECURITY SUPERVISOR   ASSISTANT MANAGER

_____
DISTRIBUTION:

_XX_DIRECTOR OF SECURITY

_XX_EXECUTIVE OFFICE

7/93

KEY CONTROL SIGN SHEET

Date_____

RING	T/O	S/O	EMPLOYEE NAME	DEPT.	T/I	S/O

2/94

PASS-ONS

DATE	TIME	INITIAL	PASS-ON	SHIFT TO DO

Appendix G

SECURITY DEPARTMENT

TRESPASS WARNING

I, the undersigned, fully understand that I have been given a warning for trespassing on private property.

I also understand that if I return to the hotel, I will be subject to arrest and prosecution by the Hotel for violating this trespass warning.

Signed:_____

Date:_____

DESCRIPTION:

Sex:_____ Height:_____ Weight:_____ Race:_____

Age:_____ Complexion:_____ Build:_____

SS#:_____ DOB:_____ Telephone:_____

Name:_____

Address:_____

Security Supervisor:_____

Date:_____

Individual Refused to sign:_____
                                        (Witness)
Date:_____

SECURITY DEPARTMENT

RADIO/KEY LOG

RADIO #	KEY #	NAME	TIME OUT	TIME IN

6/93

DATE: ___ / ___ / ___

DAY: _____

LOST AND FOUND PROPERTY SHEET

FOUND PROPERTY NUMBER:_____

REPORT TAKEN: DAY:_____ DATE:_____ TIME:_____

ARTICLE DESCRIPTION:_____

_____

_____

FOUND/LOST BY:_____

ADDRESS:_____

CHECK IN:_____ CHECK OUT:_____ ROOM NUMBER:_____

LOCATION WHERE FOUND/LOST:_____

WHEN FOUND/LOST: DAY:_____ DATE:_____ TIME:_____

DETAILS:_____

_____

_____

REPORT TAKEN BY S/O:_____ S/S_____

ARTICLE CLAIMED BY:_____

ADDRESS OF CLAIMANT:_____

RELEASING OFFICER OR SUPERVISOR:_____

DAY RELEASED:_____ DATE RELEASED:_____ TIME:_____

THIS ARTICLE HAS BEEN YELLOWED OUT OF THE FOUND PROPERTY LOG
AND/OR THE NON-LIABILITY LOG BOOK (circle one):   YES   NO

6/93

FIRE DRILL REPORT

Incident #_____

Date:_____   Shift:_____   Time:_____

Command Center Notified By:
____Telephone
____Manual Pull-Station   Location of Device:_____
____Smoke Detector
____Heat Detector   _____
____Water-flow Switch
____Tamper Switch

Zone Alarm Sounded	Yes	No
General Alarm Sounded	Yes	No
Building Evacuation Conducted	Yes	No
Fire Department Participated	Yes	No

Time of Fire Department Arrival:_____

Time all Emergency Response Team Members Arrived on Scene_____

Were Emergency Response bags brought to the scene?   Yes____   No____
Comment:_____

_____

Mark (x) as Appropriate:

Command Center (PABX) Log Attached	Yes	No
Elevator Responded	Yes	No
Fireman's Key Utilized	Yes	No
Pressurization Fans Activated	Yes	No
HVAC in Zone Shutdown	Yes	No
Smoke Exhaust Activated	Yes	No
Fire Pump Tested	Yes	No
Emergency Generator Tested	Yes	No
Emergency Communication Tested	Yes	No
Fire Department Contact Posted	Yes	No

Comment on Response:_____

_____

Corrective Measures:_____

_____

Personnel Participating: _____   _____

_____   _____   _____

Alarm Reset	Yes	No
Personnel Notified of All Clear	Yes	No
Elevators Returned to Normal	Yes	No
Pressurization Fans Shutdown	Yes	No
HVAC Activated	Yes	No

Name of Person Conducting Drill (Signature):_____

Name of Assistant Manager on Duty:_____

Bibliography

Black's Law Dictionary. Fifth edition. St. Paul: West Publishing Co., 1979.

Bleser, David M. "Security Training; Cost Effective or Not?" Unpublished study, University of South Carolina, 1995.

Brislin, Ralph F. *Effective Report Writing for Security Personnel*. Boston, MA: Butterworth-Heinemann, 1994.

Compliance Magazine. Bi-monthly. Liberty, IL: IHS Publishing Group, Nov/Dec 1994.

Crowe, Timothy D. *Crime Prevention Through Environmental Design*. Boston, MA: Butterworth-Heinemann, 1991.

Dalton, Dennis R. *Security Management: Business Strategies for Success*. Boston, MA: Butterworth-Heinemann, 1995.

Dynamics. Bi-monthly. Arlington, VA: American Society for Industrial Security, May/June 1994.

Fischer, Robert J. *Introduction to Security*. 4th ed. Stoneham, MA: Butterworth Publishers, 1987.

Lender, Mark E., and Martin, James K. *Drinking in America*. New York, NY: Macmillan Publishing Co., 1987.

Lodging. Monthly. New York, NY, July 1994.

Merriam Webster's Collegiate Dictionary, Tenth Edition. Springfield, Mass.: Merriam-Webster, 1994.

Morn, Frank. *The Eye That Never Sleeps: The History of the Pinkerton National Detective Agency.* Bloomington, IN: Indiana University Press, 1982.

NFPA. *Fire Protection Handbook.* Quincy, MA: National Fire Protection Association, 1981.

Private Security: Report of the Task Force on Private Security. Washington, DC: National Advisory Committee on Criminal Justice Standards and Goals, 1976.

Risk Management. Monthly. New York, NY: RIMS, November 1994.

Salmen, John P.S. *Accommodating All Guests: The Americans with Disabilities Act and the Lodging Industry.* Washington, DC: The American Hotel & Motel Association, 1992.

Security. Monthly. Des Plaines, IL: Cahners, July 1994.

Security Management. A Special Access Control Supplement. Arlington, VA: ASIS, November 1990.

Sennewald, Charles A. *Effective Security Management.* 2nd ed. Stoneham, MA: Butterworth Publishers, 1985.

Walsh, Timothy J. *Protection of Assets Manuals.* Santa Monica, CA: The Merritt Company, 1991.

Index